QUIT GETTING STIFFED

QU_T

GETTING

$TIFFED

A Texas Contractor's Guide to Collections and Lien Rights

KARALYNN CROMEENS

LIONCREST
PUBLISHING

Lily, Holly, and Jessy: you are my joy. I hope I have taught you that absolutely anything is possible with prayer and a whole lot of hustle. I love you all so much.

Xoxoxox

Mom

CONTENTS

INTRODUCTION

How long could you stay in business without getting paid?

I don't know about you, but I really do not want to find out. The whole point of this book is so you will never have to answer that question.

Maybe this sounds familiar: it's Wednesday, you have butterflies in your stomach, and you are feeling very anxious due to the fact that payment on your big project is over sixty days late. If it does not come in by noon tomorrow, you have no idea how you are going to make payroll. Your mind starts racing, searching for any other options; your hands are sweaty, and all your muscles are tense as you realize there is no other way to make payroll this week if that check does not come. You ask your assistant for the tenth time today if the mail has come or if she has heard anything from the general contractor who owes you for the big project. She says no to both for the tenth time. Maybe you should call the general contractor's office and demand to know where the payment is, but you don't want to be labeled as one of those "difficult to work with" contractors who has less of a chance of getting hired on the next project. What do you do? Follow the collection strategies in this book and know your rights, and you won't get stuck in a situation like this one.

For the readers of this book, this familiar situation will now be just a horror story they tell around the campfire and no longer their reality. The contractors who read this book know their rights and take the actions required to protect those rights; because of this, they are paid on time. The only butterflies they get are when they imagine how big their futures can be because they are getting paid.

WHAT YOU'LL LEARN

With helpful timelines and anecdotes, you will learn how to protect your rights to be paid the money you are owed. Applied knowledge is power—the rules this book gives offer clear instructions on the actions you must take to protect your rights. This book is written for the Texas contractor; each state has its own specific rules for liens and collections. Specifically, I will break down into bite-sized understandable terms the following topics:

- Credit in the Construction Industry
- The First Step to Having a Valid Lien
- Notices, Notices, Notices
- How to File a Valid Lien: Homesteads and Residential Projects
- How to File a Valid Lien: Commercial Projects
- The Lien Form
- How to File a Valid Bond Claim: Work Done for a Texas Governmental Entity
- What Claims Do I Have on a Federal Project?
- I Did Not Get Paid; Can I Take My Stuff Back?
- Specially Fabricated Materials
- How to Collect Retainage Every Time
- How to Enforce Your Lien
- Common Defenses to Liens
- Bonds on Private Projects
- Lien Waivers and Lien Releases
- How to Create a Consistent Collection Strategy

I can teach you about this because I have lived it. I have lived as an attorney for my clients, but I have also lived as the one trying to make payroll—the one who knows the success or failure of their business was in someone else's hands completely. I hated that feeling. I hated the butterflies, and I hated the worry about things that I could not control. So, through trial and error, I learned the rules and how to use them. When my husband and I started a material supply company, it became a necessity to learn these rules to protect our money. So that is what I did, and now I share that knowledge with you. I have been a licensed attorney in the state of Texas since 2004, but before that, I grew up in a family of contractors. I felt the stress and anxiety they had to deal with because they did not know the things you are about to learn. You learn and view things more personally when you have felt the pain you are fighting so hard to prevent. I have felt your pain, and this book is my personal story of how I learned to fix it.

What are you waiting for? Let's dive in. The first thing to understand for your successful collection strategy is how credit works in the construction industry, which is what will be broken down in Chapter 1.

CHAPTER 1

————

CREDIT IN THE CONSTRUCTION INDUSTRY

WHAT A MECHANIC'S AND MATERIALMAN'S LIEN IS AND WHY IT MATTERS

Although I had been filing mechanic's and materialman's liens ("liens") for clients for a few years, I never took the time to understand what a lien was and why they are so very important. That was until I had my very first jury trial, and I had to explain a lien to the jury—to six people who did not know anything about construction, let alone liens.

The idea for liens in the United States came from Thomas Jefferson. Jefferson wanted to encourage tradesmen to come work in the new capital of Washington. A lien is a way for a contractor and a material supplier to secure their right to payment for the labor and materials provided to the property. Said another way, contractors and material suppliers are granted an ownership interest in the property they are improving with their labor and materials. The lien is filed against the property and says that the person who filed the lien has an interest in the property to the extent that they are unpaid for labor and/ or materials supplied to the property.

The entire construction industry runs on credit. Knowing the definition of a lien is essential to running a profitable business.

THE CONSTRUCTION INDUSTRY RUNS ON CREDIT

You work, you put out money to pay your guys and to pay for equipment and materials, and then you have to wait to get paid. You are extending the general contractor and the owner credit when you work first and get paid later. The general contractor and owner are in debt to you for the value of your work and/or materials.

There are two types of credit/debt: secured and unsecured. Which do you think you would rather have?

Secured, correct. You want the money you are owed to be secured by an asset. For example, when the bank gives you a loan to buy your house, the money you owe the bank is secured by a lien on your house. If you do not pay the bank, they can enforce that lien by mandating the sale of your house to pay the amount you owe them. A lien you file against a project does the same thing for the amount you are owed. The amount you are owed is secured by the property when you file a lien, meaning you could enforce your lien by forcing the sale of the property to pay you the amount you are owed.

The other kind of credit/debt is unsecured. This is like credit card debt. There is no asset to secure the amount owed. This is what you have if you do not file a lien; you have the right to collect the money you are owed from the general contractor or whoever hired you to do the work, but you do not have an interest in the property. When you file a lien, you have both a secured claim against the property and unsecured claim against the general contractor or whoever hired you to work.

WHAT IS A LIEN?

A lien is the vehicle used to make the amounts you are owed a secured debt. A lien is a piece of paper filed in the real property records that says, "Hey, I have an interest in this property because I have not been paid for my labor or the materials I used to improve the property." It is a public record, there for the world to see.

HOW A LIEN WORKS

The owner of a property does not want anyone else to have an interest in their property. If there are liens on their property, it means someone else has an interest in the property and the owner does not own 100% of their property. An owner cannot sell what they do not own and therefore cannot sell 100% of their property until all the liens are taken care of and released. So, before an owner can sell their property, they need to make sure it's free and clear of all liens.

One of my favorite things to see is the name of a title company on the caller ID at the office. This means one of my client's liens is going to be paid. The first step in the sale of a property is for the buyer and seller to enter into a contract for the sale of the property. During this contract phase, the buyer requires the seller to prove they own 100% of the property they are selling. The seller does this by providing the buyer a title report from a title company. This title report will list anything that affects the seller's 100% ownership interest; specifically, it will list any liens against the property. For a seller to sell 100% of the property, they must resolve any liens listed on the title report. My firm's name and number are on the lien, so the title company will call my office to find out exactly how much my client is owed to get a release of their lien, and the sale of the property can proceed.

WHAT DO YOU HAVE WITHOUT A LIEN?

Without a lien, all you have is a breach of contract claim against the general contractor or whoever hired you. The real leverage to ensure payment is having a lien against the owner's property. The owner is the general contractor's customer, and you know everyone likes to keep their customers happy. A lien on their customer's property will not make them happy. When you file a lien, you can sue the owner to enforce the lien, and you still have your breach of contract claim against the general contractor or whoever hired you. If you have a lien, even if the general contractor goes out of business, you will still be paid by the owner.

WHO CAN FILE A LIEN?

Anyone who improves the value of the property with their labor and/or materials has the right to have a lien. This includes but is not limited to: material suppliers, tradespeople, contractors, architects, engineers, surveyors, landscapers, and demolition crews.

CONSTITUTIONAL VERSUS STATUTORY LIENS

There are two different types of liens: constitutional and statutory. A constitutional lien, as the name implies, comes straight from the Texas Constitution. Anyone who is hired directly by an owner to provide labor and materials to their property will have a constitutional lien. Constitutional liens have several benefits that we will discuss in Chapter 2. A statutory lien is what everyone who improves property and is not hired directly by an owner has. Statutory liens have very specific rules that must be followed for the lien to be valid. We will discuss these rules in detail in Chapters 6 and 9.

WHAT A SHAM CONTRACT IS, AND WHY IT MATTERS

A sham contract is a mechanism that allows you to have a constitutional lien, even if you don't have an agreement directly with the owner. If the owner and the general contractor are the same person, you can still have a constitutional lien. When this normally applies is when the property is owned by one company and the general contractor is a different company, but the same person owns or controls both companies. When one person owns or controls both the property and the general contractor, the contract between them is considered a "sham contract," and the law says that you have a constitutional lien and do not have to comply with all the requirements of a statutory lien.

I once had a client who was a painting contractor, Jason. Jason was just starting out, and he did a good job and took great pride in his work. Jason's biggest and only client at the time was a spec home builder, Huge Homebuilder ("Huge"). Huge was building five different communities all at the same time, and Jason was their interior painter. Jason was paid by the square foot plus materials. The relationship was going well; Huge was a little slow to pay, but there were no big issues. After about a year, Jason started to notice he was always broke at the price he was charging. He should have been making decent money—not anything crazy, but enough not to be broke. After some investigation, Jason discovered that Huge was shorting the square footage they paid him for. Jason would never double-check the square footage he was being paid for; he just trusted that Huge would pay him the right amount. After a review of all of the work he had done for Huge over the last year, it turned out Jason had been shorted over $100,000. He came to my office on the verge of a mental breakdown and had no idea what to do.

After a review of all of the information, I formulated a plan, and it was one of my best. Turns out that Huge did not own any of the properties that Jason worked on; rather, all of the properties were owned by different companies that had the same name as the subdivision. At first glance, it appeared that Jason did not have any lien rights because he was not hired by the owner and did not send timely notice. But upon further investigation, it turned out that the same people who owned Huge owned each of the subdivisions, so the contract between Huge and the owners was a sham contract. Jason therefore had constitutional liens on all of the properties he had worked on. Jason could only have valid liens on the houses that had not sold (more on that in Chapter 2). It was over fifty liens in three different counties, but we filed them all. We also filed a lawsuit to foreclose the liens and claims against Huge for the amount owed on houses that we could not file liens against.

Almost every day, we got a call from a title company that one of the houses we had liened was going to closing. They needed to know how much Jason was owed so they could make sure he was paid in full for that property and release the lien. At the end of the day, Jason got everything he was owed. It was a long road, but it was worth it. Jason had leverage because of the liens he could file due to the sham contract between Huge and the owners of the properties.

WHERE LIENS NEED TO BE FILED

Liens attach to the property where the work was done, so the affidavit claiming a lien must be filed in the county where the property is located. Specifically, liens are filed in the real property records. If a property is in more than one county, the lien needs to be filed in the county where a majority of the property is located. When I file a lien against a property that is in more than one county, I will file it in both counties just to be safe.

YOU NEED THE HELP OF A QUALIFIED ATTORNEY

You cannot just file your lien. To have a properly perfected lien, you will need the help of a competent attorney. There are steps that you can take along the way to decrease the attorney's involvement, but to do it correctly, you will need to hire an attorney that is familiar with liens. If your lien is invalid, not only will you not get paid the money you are owed, but you may have to pay attorney fees incurred to remove your lien or even a $10,000 penalty for filing a fraudulent lien.

WHAT IS REQUIRED TO HAVE A VALID LIEN IS DIFFERENT IN ALL FIFTY STATES

The requirements for a valid lien are different in all fifty states, so those lien packages you can buy online that are the same no matter what state you live in most likely will not get you a valid lien in the state of Texas. Texas has some of the most complicated rules for filing a valid lien. You may think that you are saving money filing a lien with an online service, but in most cases, any liens they file are invalid, and you will not only lose that money but also have to pay someone else's attorney fees.

Not all attorneys know how to file a valid lien, so you need to interview law firms before you hire one. The attorney that prepared your will is not the one you want to file your lien. Ask the firm what their collection strategy is. Is it just sending letters and filing liens, or will they make phone calls? Ask them how successful they are at collecting liens without filing a lawsuit. Ask how often you will be updated on the status of your file. Ask how fast they return phone calls. Interview a few firms and find the one that is the best fit for your company.

I had a long-time client that thought they could save money by using an online lien-filing service for a project for which they were owed $30,000. They used the service and filed the lien, then called my office to file the lawsuit to enforce the lien. After a complete review of all the documents provided by the lien-filing service, we told the client we would not recommend filing a lawsuit to enforce the lien. The lien was filed late, and the notice was not sent properly. Because of this, the lien was invalid. We were able to collect the amount the client was owed via other collection strategies, but they had given up valuable leverage by failing to have a lien.

Liens are great leverage when done properly. When done

incorrectly, they are a liability. The first step to understanding what it takes to have a valid lien in Texas is knowing your place and project type, which I will explain in the next chapter.

KEY TAKEAWAYS

- The construction industry runs on credit. Secure your right to be paid for the work you do with a properly filed lien.
- There are two types of liens: constitutional and statutory.
- When the owner and the general contractor are the same person, it is a sham contract, and you will have a constitutional lien.
- Liens need to be filed with the county clerk in the county where the property is located.
- You need an attorney who is familiar with liens to file your lien.

CHAPTER 2

THE FIRST STEP TO HAVING A VALID LIEN

KNOWING YOUR PLACE AND TYPE OF PROJECT

"I don't understand. Why is my lien invalid?" Martha from Super Land Clearing Subcontractor (SLCS) asked me. Martha had received a letter from an attorney demanding she remove a lien that she had filed on a day care project she was owed money on. The day care was being sold, and the title company had made the current owner aware of SLCS's lien. The lien needed to be taken care of before the sale could go through. The owner's attorney had sent a letter to Martha demanding that the lien be removed immediately because it was holding up the sale. The owner threatened that if she refused to remove the lien, she would be responsible for the damages the owner suffered due to the loss of the sale of the day care and attorney fees. Martha had found a lien form online, filled it out, and filed it with the county clerk. The lien was completely invalid because no notices of any kind had been sent and the lien was extremely late in being filed. Although SLCS was actually due the $50,000 claimed in the lien, the lien was invalid and needed to be removed immediately. If the owner lost the sale of the day care because Martha refused to release the lien, she would be liable for any damages the owner suffered because of the loss of the sale, which could be in the hundreds of thousands of dollars. The general contractor had filed bankruptcy, and this lien was the only hope Martha had of getting paid. Unfortunately, Martha had to release SLCS's lien and was not paid the $50,000 she was owed for that project. If SLCS's lien had been valid, the owner would have had to pay the lien before the day care could be sold. The best thing I could do was to partner with Martha and her company to show them how to perfect their liens in the future.

It is extremely important to understand your lien rights and what you need to do to protect them. Could your company handle a $50,000 loss like Martha's?

Knowing the type of your project and your place in the construction food chain is the first step to knowing the correct actions you will need to take to perfect your lien or bond claim.

Construction Food Chain Chart

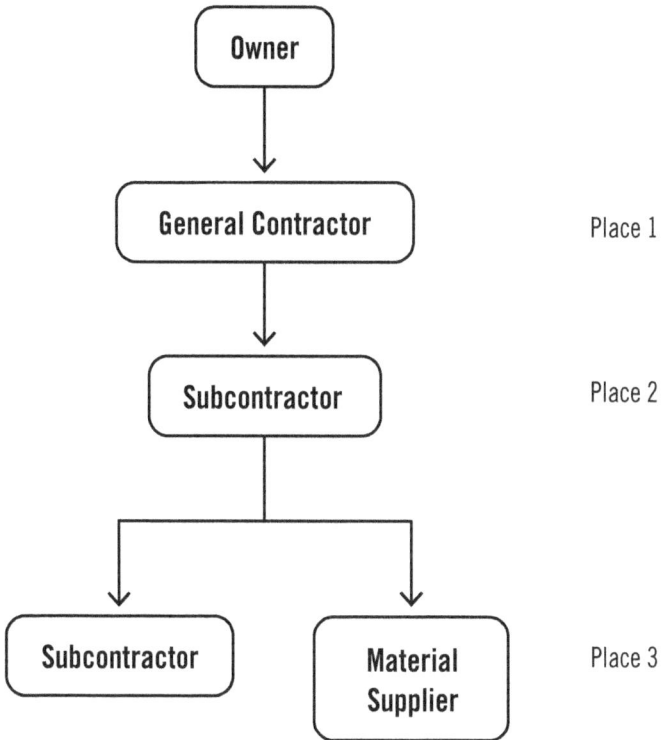

```
                    ┌─────────────┐
                    │    Owner    │
                    └──────┬──────┘
                           │
                           ▼
              ┌────────────────────────┐
              │   General Contractor   │          Place 1
              └───────────┬────────────┘
                          │
                          ▼
              ┌────────────────────────┐
              │      Subcontractor     │          Place 2
              └───────────┬────────────┘
              ┌───────────┴───────────┐
              ▼                       ▼
    ┌──────────────────┐   ┌──────────────────┐
    │  Subcontractor   │   │     Material     │    Place 3
    │                  │   │     Supplier     │
    └──────────────────┘   └──────────────────┘
```

KNOW YOUR PLACE

When you contract directly with the owner, you have a constitutional lien, as granted by the Texas constitution.

This is Place 1. There are very few actions you must take when you are in Place 1 to perfect your liens. Anyone can be in Place 1; it does not matter if you are normally in Place 3 or below. If you are hired by the owner of the property, you will be in Place 1.

FIRST ACTION

The first action you must take to begin the perfection of your lien or bond claim depends on your place in the construction food chain. You are considered to be in Place 2 when you have a contract directly with the general contractor (the contractor hired by the owner). Contractors are normally in Place 2 and will have more time than those in Place 3 to make the first move to perfect their lien or bond claim.

Anyone who does work for or supplies materials to a contractor that is hired by the general contractor is considered to be in Place 3. It doesn't matter if you are in Place 3 or further down the chain; everyone who is not in direct contract with a contractor hired by the general contractor is considered in Place 3 for purposes of lien and bond claims. The people in Place 3 will have to act sooner to perfect their lien or bond claims than those in Place 2.

PROJECT TYPE

The second part of knowing when you must take action to perfect your lien or bond claim is knowing the type of project you are working on. In the state of Texas, there are five different types of projects to consider when talking about lien and bond claims:

- **Homestead.** A residential property that is owned by the same people who are living in it on a full-time basis. An individual or married couple can only have one homestead at a time.
- **Residential.** A single-family house, duplex, triplex, or quadruplex owned by one or more individual persons. One or more of the owners lives in the building.
- **Commercial.** All projects that are not residential, homestead, or public.
- **Texas public works.** A project contracted for or owned by a Texas governmental entity.
- **Federal project.** A project contracted for or owned by a federal governmental entity.

Each one of these project types has different requirements to have a valid lien or bond claim. We will dive into when you need to take action and what actions to take to perfect your lien and bond claims very specifically by project type in Chapter 7. The important thing to note is if you miss the first required step, you can't include one month's worth of labor/materials on your lien and bond claims.

It is very important to know what project type you're dealing with when you begin working. I had a client who was a drywall contractor, knew the lien timelines, and would send out the first notice on his own, and then my office would file the lien. One month, he sent over a library project he had not been paid on and wanted us to file a lien. We had to let the client know that you cannot file a lien on a library because it is publicly owned. He had not sent the required notice to the bond company, so he did not have a bond claim either. He was owed $10,000, but he was never paid by the general contractor. In the end, he decided it was not worth the time and money it would cost to file a lawsuit against the general contractor and just walked away from the money he was owed. Had this client filed a timely bond claim, he would have created leverage and been paid promptly. Because he did not know that the library was a public works project, he missed the deadline to send the required letters. This is why it is important to understand what type of project you are working on in the beginning.

OWNERS AND GENERAL CONTRACTORS KNOW YOUR LIEN AND BOND CLAIM DEADLINES

Do not ever assume that the general contractor or owner that is promising a check next week is not aware of your lien or bond claim timelines. I have had plenty of clients come into my office and want to file a lien, but they are too late because the general contractor or owner promised to pay them but never did. In other words, the general contractor or owner never planned on paying them but kept making promises of payment so the contractor would miss the lien or bond claim deadlines by failing to take action when required.

Knowing your deadline to take action to perfect your lien or bond claim gives you power and leverage. When a general contractor or owner is promising payment, you do not have to argue. You can believe their promises and also make sure you follow the steps to perfect your lien or bond claim. Like Ronald Reagan said, "Trust, but verify." In this case, trust but take the actions required to protect your rights.

THE ONLY TIME YOUR PLACE AND TYPE DON'T MATTER: CONSTITUTIONAL LIENS

"What do you mean I can still file a lien? It's been six months since I finished that project, and I did not send any notice," Kelly from Super Plumbing Subcontractor (SPS) said to me. Kelly was hired by General Contractor Inc. to perform plumbing work at a project owned by Owner Inc. After some research, I was able to determine that both General Contractor Inc. and Owner Inc. were owned and controlled by John Doe. Because Mr. Doe owned and controlled both companies and the contract between the two companies would be considered a sham contract, as far as lien rights go, SPS had a constitutional lien and could file its lien at any time before Owner Inc. sold the property.

You have a constitutional lien when you are in Place 1 or there is a sham contract between Place 1 and Place 2.

How to Have a Constitutional Lien

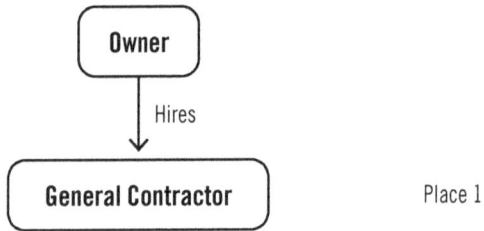

```
        ┌──────────────┐
        │    Owner     │
        └──────────────┘
               │ Hires
               ↓
  ┌─────────────────────────┐
  │   General Contractor    │          Place 1
  └─────────────────────────┘
```

Anyone who is hired directly by the Owner is consider a General Contractor.
The contract does not have to be in writing unless the property is a homestead.

NO NOTICE REQUIRED

If you are a Place 1 contractor, you do not have to send any of the notices required for statutory liens. There are no timelines governing when a constitutional lien must be filed. You can file a constitutional lien at any time as long as it is before the owner who hired you sells the property. A constitutional lien will not be enforced against a new owner of the property if it was not filed before the property was sold. The constitutional lien needs to be filed with the county clerk in the county where the property is located.

Learn the lesson Martha learned without it costing you $50,000. If Martha had properly perfected SLCS's lien rights, she would have gotten paid. Know what is required to have a valid lien and never miss a deadline. In the next chapter, we will go over notice, which is the first action you must take to have a valid lien or bond claim.

KEY TAKEAWAYS

- The first step in protecting your lien rights is knowing your place.
- The next step is knowing which of the five types of projects you are working on.
- The general contractor and the owner know your lien deadlines. Don't let a promise of a payment to come push you outside of your deadlines!
- You have a constitutional lien if you contract directly with the owner or if there is a sham contract between the owner and general contractor. For more information about sham contracts, refer back to Chapter 1.

CHAPTER 3

———

NOTICES, NOTICES, NOTICES

There is nothing more uncomfortable than watching your client struggle when they are on the witness stand during trial and being unable to help. I had a long-time client that had to take their lien case to a jury trial. One of the big contentions the property owner's attorney had with my client's lien was that one of the notices required to have a valid lien was mailed missing a zero in the address. The attorney kept asking my client very battering questions like: "Where did you get this address? This address is wrong, correct? How can you expect a letter with a wrong address to get to the right person? How could you miss the fact that the address was missing a zero? How is it fair to have a lien on someone else's property if you did not even send the notice letter to the correct address?"

I promise you, from that moment on, that client triple-checked every letter they would ever send out to make sure the address was 100% correct. Do not get me wrong: we still won that case. The property owner had a few different places they received mail, and luckily, my client had sent the notice to all the addresses.

WHY IS NOTICE SO IMPORTANT?

Sending timely and proper notices is the key to perfecting your lien rights. Why are all these notices required? Having a lien on someone's property is a very extreme remedy; like I said before, you can also force the sale of the property to satisfy your lien. Think about it: an owner has no idea who any of the second- or third-place contractors or material suppliers are, yet any of these contractors could file a lien on their property. Notices give the owner and the general contractor a chance to make sure any unpaid party is paid. Specifically, the first notice that is sent out gives the general contractor a chance to take care of the nonpayment issue before they pay the contractor and before their customer—the owner—finds out there is an issue. The second notice gives the owner a chance to take care of the nonpayment issue before they pay the general contractor or before a lien is filed against their property.

For example, Super Plumbing Subcontractor (SPS) falls

behind on its payment to its material supplier, Plumbing Supply. Plumbing Supply knows that in order to perfect its lien, the first notice it must send is to SPS's general contractor. Plumbing Supply sends the general contractor the required notice, and the general contractor pays Plumbing Supply out of SPS's next payment. If the material supplier were late in sending the general contractor the notice, the general contractor may have already paid SPS.

There is nothing wrong with sending notice early or sending more notices than what is required by law. If you send notice as soon as you realize there is an issue, it will give all parties involved more time to resolve it. Your lien rights will be lost if you send notices late or to the wrong people.

The notices that are required are intended to let the people further up the construction food chain know that you are not being paid so they can make sure you are paid before payments are issued to those above you in the construction food chain. When timely notice is not sent, then the owner or general contractor does not get a chance to fix the situation before the payment is made. If we look at the chart from Chapter 2, we see notices let the owner and general contractor know if there is a kink in the food chain and the money is not making it to the lower places.

REQUIREMENTS FOR EFFECTIVE NOTICE

Under current Texas state law, all notices must be sent as certified mail, return receipt requested. The only way to prove that your notice was sent on or before the required date is to take it to the post office and have the receipt stamped.

I recommend putting all of your certified numbers on the actual letters you are sending out. That way, you can easily tell which certified receipt goes with which letter.

Without the post office stamp, the date you sent the letter can be questioned. As a matter of course, if you have an email address for the recipient, send the notices via email too. You can never give too much notice.

The notice is effective when it is sent to the correct address with the proper amount of postage. It does not matter if it is actually signed for by the person you sent it to. If you have done everything in your power to ensure the person entitled to notice received it, they cannot get out of the effect of the notice by not picking up or refusing their certified mail.

The only way to prove that effective and timely notice was sent is to have the stamped receipt. What happens if you don't have this receipt? Then you can't prove you sent effective and timely notice, and your lien will be invalid. I represented a lumber supply company that had used an online lien filing service to file a lien on a project for which they were owed $50,000. Once the lien was filed, they received a letter from the owner's attorney asking for all the documentation that said their lien was valid. The lumber company sent the owner's attorney everything the lien filing service provided them, but there was no stamped receipt from the post office verifying when their notices were sent. At the post office website, you can check the history of the certified letter; according to the website, my client's letters that needed to be sent on the 15th of the month were not entered into the post office system until the 17th of the month. That was all it took. The post office website saying the letter was not mailed on time and having no evidence to the contrary (like a stamped receipt) meant the lien was invalid and the $50,000 was gone. A lien can have a lot of leverage, but to get that leverage, you need to follow each step exactly as the law requires.

ACTUAL NOTICE

Another way to prove notice under the law is to prove someone actually knew that you were owed money. I would not rely on this type of notice, but it can work in some situations. An example of this is when you send your pay application to the general contractor via email, and they send back a verification that it was received. The general contractor now has actual knowledge of how much you are claiming you are owed for the month of the pay application. You can also give notice by personal delivery, but if you are going to give notice this way, bring a witness with you.

WHO IS ENTITLED TO NOTICE?

Notices need to be sent to the owner and the general contractor. Unless you have a contract directly with them, you may not know their addresses. Below is a list of resources you can use to find the correct addresses. When you use these resources, print the page you get your information from and put it in your file. If there is a question about the address you sent notice to later, it is great evidence to prove that it was a valid address.

- **Texas Secretary of State**. The SOS is the best place to find an address for a business registered in Texas, but you need to have an account and it is a dollar per search. **direct.sos.state.tx.us**

- **Texas Comptroller.** This has a free search function for a business registered in Texas, but it is not as updated as the SOS. **comptroller.texas.gov/taxes/ franchise/**
- **Public Data.** This is a subscription-based website that lets you search for driver license information, which is the best way to find an address for a person.
- **County Tax Records.** Every county in Texas has an appraisal district website that lists all the properties in that county. Most counties have this information available online for free. Normally you can search by owner name or address of the property to find out who owns the property and a current mailing address.
- **County Assumed Name Records.** If a business is a Doing Business As (DBA) and has filed with the county, those records are public information. Most counties have the information available online for free.
- **County Real Property Records.** Every county keeps records of every transaction dealing with real property. Most counties have these records online.
- **Google.** If none of the above work, you can try Google, but it is not as reliable as the other resources.

TIMELINES FOR NOTICES

Another huge mistake I find when dealing with lien claimants is when the timeline to send the required notices begins. The common misconception is that the timeline to send notices starts from the date of the last work done, when the opposite is actually true. The timeline to send notice starts from the first month for which you are owed money. For example, if you are owed money for work done in January, February, and March, your timeline to send notice starts in January, not March. If you start your lien notice timeline from March, you will be late for the work done in January and February.

Another misconception is that you must file a lien for each month you are owed money. This is not true. You can keep sending notices for each month that you are owed money, but do not file the lien until your work or the project is complete, whichever comes first.

EACH MONTH MUST MEET ITS OWN REQUIREMENTS

Under Texas law, the lien process is broken up by months, which makes sense because a construction project is broken up by months. Every month, you submit your pay application to the general contractor; in turn, the general contractor submits its pay application to the owner every month. The owner pays the general contractor for a month at a time based on their pay application.

The notice timelines all start from the first month for which you are owed money, not the last. Each month for which you are owed money must meet all the notice requirements. If you are owed money for work done in January, February, and March, you must be able to prove you have provided timely notice for all work done in January, you must prove you have given timely notice for the work done in February, and you must prove you have sent timely notice for your work done in March. Each month must stand on its own.

INVOICE DATE DOES NOT MATTER

The timeline for notices starts when you actually did the work or provided the materials, not your invoice date. Let me explain with an example. Super Brick Supplier (SBS) delivers materials to an office building project site on October 30. In accordance with SBS's process, the invoice is not created and sent out until November 2. The timeline for SBS to send notice starts in October because that is when the materials were delivered, not the day the invoice was issued.

I have seen many liens be invalidated on this premise. What happens is that the contractor or material supplier will review their open invoice report to determine for what projects notice needs to be sent. Using the example above, SBS reviews its open invoice report in December and does not send any notice for the office building project mentioned above because those invoices are listed as

November invoices. December 15 passes, but SBS does not send notice to the general contractor for the office building project that they are owed money for materials delivered in October. SBS has now lost their lien rights for materials delivered in October. There is nothing that SBS can do to get the lien rights back for October. But if they follow the correct process for materials delivered after October, they will have lien rights for those materials.

SEND NOTICE EARLY AND OFTEN

You do not lose any rights if you send notice early, and you can send multiple months in the same notice. Using the example above, suppose SBS supplied materials in October, November, and December. The first notice required is December 15; by this time, SBS knows what materials were supplied in November, so they could have October and November invoices in the same notice. Then there would be no need to send another notice in January for the November invoices.

It is best practice to include the full amount that you are owed in all of your notices. You can break it down by month, but be sure to include the full amount. This way, whatever notice is actually received, they are aware of the full amount that you are owed.

HOLIDAYS AND WEEKENDS

The law does not care if your notice deadline falls on a holiday or a weekend when the post office is closed. In other words, if your deadline to send notice falls on a holiday or a weekend, you must send your notice before that date. No extra time is added on just because the post office is closed.

You do not want to learn the importance of sending proper notice on the witness stand. When you send out notices, do the research to find a good address, put that research in your file, and triple-check the address on every letter that goes out. Another important aspect of having a valid lien is whether the property is a homestead or not. We will cover that sticky situation in the next chapter.

KEY TAKEAWAYS

- Do the research to find the correct address to send notice, and keep that research in your file.
- Triple-check the addresses on all the letters you send out.
- Take the letter to the post office to be stamped when you send it out.
- If your notice deadline falls on a weekend or a holiday, make sure you send it out before that date.
- Each month must meet its own notice requirements.
- There is nothing wrong with sending notice early and often.

CHAPTER 4

———

HOW TO FILE A VALID LIEN

HOMESTEADS AND RESIDENTIAL PROJECTS

"Filing my contract in the real property records sounds like a lot of work to have a lien on a house for my $500 invoice," said Rachel from Super AC Subcontractor. She had come to my office to find out if liens would be an effective way to collect money she was owed. Rachel's company did mostly repairs to residential AC units, and her average invoice was $1,000 or less. With all the steps required to have a valid lien on a homestead, it was not worth Rachel's time or money to make filing liens part of her collection process. I helped Rachel with some other things she could do to make sure she was paid what she was owed; you can learn more about these strategies in Chapter 16.

Texas protects homesteads at all costs. There is therefore a very extensive process to follow to have a lien on a homestead.

WHEN IS A PROPERTY CONSIDERED A HOMESTEAD?

What is a homestead under the law? When an individual or couple owns the property where they reside a majority of the time, that property is a homestead. An individual or a couple can only have one homestead at a time. A homestead cannot be owned by a company.

The definition of the property is determined at the time construction begins. If the owner had a different homestead at the time the construction of residence began, then it is not considered a homestead, even if the intention is to use the residence as their homestead once construction is complete. The intent to make a house your homestead does not make that house your homestead if you already have a homestead.

I once represented a material supplier who was owed $20,000 for materials supplied to a high-end house that was being remodeled. When the remodel started, the owners were living in a different house they owned, but before the remodel was complete, they had moved into the high-end house. They refused to pay my client because my client had not complied with all the requirements to have a lien on a homestead. I relayed on my client's behalf that they were not required to follow the requirements for a homestead because the high-end house was not the owners' homestead when the project began. For a project to be considered a homestead for lien purposes, it must be their homestead when the construction began. They disagreed with my reasoning, and the dispute went to trial. At trial, my client won. The court agreed with my legal argument that the property had to be a homestead at the time construction began.

HOW TO HAVE A LIEN ON A HOMESTEAD

The first step to have a perfected lien on a homestead is having the owner sign a contract for the work you will be doing. The contract must state what you are doing and the amount you agreed to for the work. It must be signed by the owner before the work begins. If the property is owned by a married couple, both of them must sign the contract. Before you can file a lien, this contract must be filed in the real property records in the county where the property is located. There is no requirement that the contract be filed of record before the work begins, but it must be filed before you file a lien.

The Texas property code also has a disclosure statement that is required to be given to the owner before the residential construction contract is signed. You can find a copy of this disclosure at **subcontractorinstitute.com**. The Texas property code also requires you to provide the owners with the list of contractors and suppliers who will be working on the residence. This must also be provided before construction begins. You can find a form to fill out that provides the owners with this information at **subcontractorinstitute.com**. Although the property code requires these to be given to the owner, failure to do so will not make your lien invalid.

NOT HIRED BY THE OWNER

What happens when you are a contractor to the contractor hired by the owner on a homestead project? If the contractor properly got the contract signed by all owners before the construction began, all contractors will receive the benefit of that contract. Meaning that if the contractor that was hired by the owners has lien rights, so will you; if not, then you will not have lien rights either. If you are going to work on a homestead as a contractor, you need to see the contract with the owner before you begin working. You can check the real property records to see if it has been filed there or ask the contractor that was hired by the owner to show you a copy of the signed contract. If the construction of a residence is being funded by a bank, the residential construction contract is normally part of the bank's paperwork and they will file it of record with the county clerk.

RESIDENTIAL PROJECTS

"Just because it's your house does not mean it qualifies as your homestead," I told Sammy the homeowner. Sammy had hired a contractor to build a deck on his lake house. They never signed a written contract, and now there was a dispute about how much the contractor was supposed to be paid. The contractor had threatened to file a lien on the lake house. Sammy was under the impression that contractor could not file a lien because there was not a signed contract. Only a homestead requires a signed contract to file a lien; a secondary residence like a lake house does not require a signed contract to file a lien. Neither does any other type of project. The only type of project that requires a contract in writing to file a lien is a homestead.

A residential construction project does not require a signed contract to file a lien, but it does have the same shortened timelines as a homestead project.

What is a residential construction project? It is a single-family house, duplex, triplex, quadruplex, or a unit in a multitenant structure used for residential purposes, owned by one or more individuals. The key is that the property is owned by an individual. If a property is owned by an entity, it cannot be residential or a homestead. Instead, it would be considered a commercial project. A spec house or a townhouse that is owed by a company is not a homestead or a residential project but will be classified as a commercial project.

HOW TO FIND WHO OWNS A PROPERTY

How do you find out who owns a property in order to send them notice? The only way to know for sure who owns the property is to search the property records, but to do that properly, you should hire an attorney or title company. Another reliable source is the appraisal district for the county where the property is located. They have a database that you can search by address to find the owner of a property. You could also ask the contractor that hired you who the owner of the property is.

WHEN TO SEND NOTICE FOR A HOMESTEAD OR RESIDENTIAL PROJECT

If you are a contractor on a homestead or residential project, the first notice of nonpayment that needs to be sent to perfect your lien is the 15th day of the second month after you are owed money. If you are owed money for work done in June and July, the first notice of nonpayment must be sent on or before August 15. The notice must be sent to the contractor that was hired by the owner and to the owner. You can find a form of the notice letter that must be sent at **subcontractorinstitute.com**.

Keep sending this notice for each month you are owed money for work done on the project. The next step to having a perfected lien on a homestead or residential project is to file the actual lien. The lien must be filed by the 15th day of the third month after you last worked on the project or thirty days after final completion of the homestead or residence, whichever comes first. We will get to what is required to be in a lien in Chapters 5 and 6, but do note that a lien on a homestead must have this statement in bold at the top: NOTICE: THIS IS NOT A LIEN. THIS IS ONLY AN AFFIDAVIT CLAIMING A LIEN.

If you have completed your work on the project and you are owed money for work done in June, July, and August, you must file your lien on or before November 15 or thirty days after final completion of the homestead or residence, whichever comes first.

1st month **2nd month** **3rd month**
unpaid unpaid unpaid

Month you
did the work

→ Still working?

→ **Yes**
Keep sending notices for each
month you are owed money.

→ **No**
15th day of 3rd month, file lien.

On or before 5 days of the lien
being filed, send notice of the
lien that was filed to the Owner
and General Contractor.

15th day
Send Intent to Lien letter to
General Contractor
and Owner of the property.

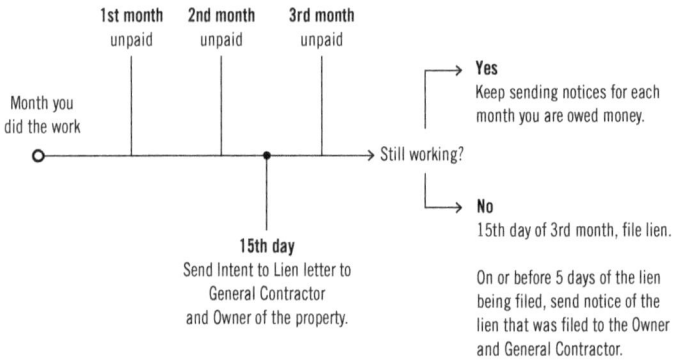

If at any time during the lien process the project is completed,
you must file your lien within 30 days.

NOTICE OF LIEN

Once the lien is filed, you must send a copy to the owner and the contractor that was hired by the owner. It does not have to be file-stamped by the clerk; it just has to be a copy of what you filed. Notice of the lien needs to be sent out within five days of the lien being filed. Just like all other notices, it must be sent as certified mail and the receipt must be stamped by the post office. **If this notice is not sent, your lien will be invalid.**

EFFECT OF LIEN ON A HOMESTEAD

Legally, you can file a lien on a homestead, but at the end

of the day, even if you get a judgment establishing your lien, you cannot kick someone out of their homestead to enforce your lien. In addition, courts don't like liens on homesteads, so even if you have done everything correctly, a court may refuse to enforce your lien or even issue an order removing your lien.

Even if you can't kick someone out of their homestead, there are other ways to collect the amount you are owed. Pay attention while the project is ongoing to any clues that would tell you where the owner banks. Once you have a judgment foreclosing your lien, you can use that judgment to garnish a bank account. Also pay attention to any clues that let you know if the owner has other assets that can be seized to satisfy your judgment. This must be a property other than their homestead, such as boats, RVs, ATVs, or extra vehicles. All of these things can be taken to satisfy your judgment.

Knowing the owner of the property and your place in the construction food chain is essential to know what you must do to protect your lien rights. This is especially true when it comes to commercial projects, which is what we will dive into in the next chapter.

KEY TAKEAWAYS

- Find out if a project is residential or a homestead before you begin.
- If it is a homestead, make sure there is a contract signed by all owners.
- The first notice of nonpayment must be sent to the contractor hired by the owner and to the owner by the 15th day of the second month after you are owed money.
- Make sure to send out a notice of the lien that was filed.

CHAPTER 5

HOW TO FILE
A VALID LIEN

COMMERCIAL PROJECTS

One of the biggest areas of my practice is construction collections, specifically liens on commercial projects. Of all the clients who come to my office to file liens, 75% of them get paid before the actual lien is filed. Between the collection phone calls and the required notices to the parties at the top of the construction food chain who do not want liens filed on their projects, we can more often than not get our clients paid without filing a lien. The owner and the general contractor know when your notices need to be sent to have a valid lien—which also means they know when your notices are late and your lien will be invalid. If the general contractor or owner knows your lien will be valid, your claim is more likely to be paid before it is actually filed.

The best lien is the one that never has to be filed. Sending timely notices lets all the parties involved know that you are aware of what is required to file a valid lien and that you will file one if you are not paid.

THE FIRST NOTICE FOR PLACE 2

A commercial project is any project that is privately owned (not owned by a government entity) that is not a homestead or residential project. As a party hired by the general contractor or second-place contractor, the first notice that you must send out is by the 15th day of the third month after you are first owed money. For example, if you are owed money for work done in March, April, and May, the first notice you must send is June 15. June is the third month after March, which is the first month you are owed money for. This notice needs to be sent to the general contractor and the owner. You can find a draft of this notice letter at **subcontractorinstitute.com**.

Timeline for Valid Texas Lien:
Place 2, Commercial Projects

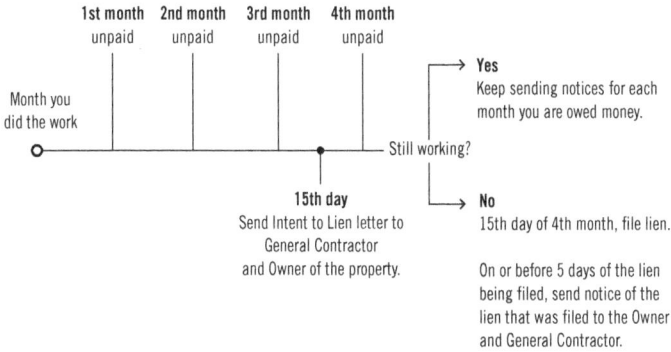

1st month	2nd month	3rd month	4th month
unpaid	unpaid	unpaid	unpaid

Month you did the work

→ **Yes**
Keep sending notices for each month you are owed money.

Still working?

15th day
Send Intent to Lien letter to General Contractor and Owner of the property.

→ **No**
15th day of 4th month, file lien.

On or before 5 days of the lien being filed, send notice of the lien that was filed to the Owner and General Contractor.

If at any time during the lien process the project is completed, you must file your lien within 30 days.

THE FIRST NOTICE FOR PLACE 3 AND BELOW

Contractors and material suppliers at Place 3 and below have lien rights as well. They must send an earlier notice than Place 2 claimants. Contractors and material suppliers in Place 3 or below must send the general contractor notice of unpaid amounts on the 15th day of the second month after they remain unpaid. Using the example from above, if a Place 3 contractor or material supplier is owed money for March, April, and May, the first notice they must send is May 15, the second month after March. This notice only needs to be sent to the general contractor. You can find a draft of this notice letter at **subcontractorinstitute.com**.

Contractors and material suppliers in Place 3 or below must also send the same notice as a Place 2 contractor. If a contractor or material supplier remains unpaid after they send the second-month notice, they must send notice to the general contractor and owner by the 15th day of the third month. Using the example from the previous paragraph, the Place 3 contractor or material supplier is due for March, April, and May. They must send notice to the owner and general contractor on or before June 15. It is the same notice that is sent by Place 2 and can be found at **subcontractorinstitute.com.**

Timeline for Valid Texas Lien:
Place 3, Commercial Projects

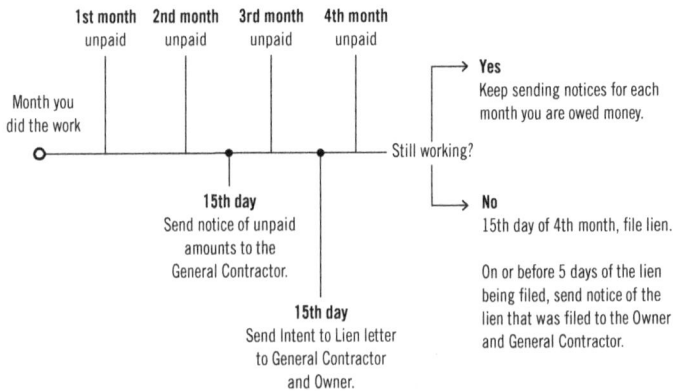

| | 1st month unpaid | 2nd month unpaid | 3rd month unpaid | 4th month unpaid |

Month you did the work

Yes
Keep sending notices for each month you are owed money.

Still working?

15th day
Send notice of unpaid amounts to the General Contractor.

No
15th day of 4th month, file lien.

On or before 5 days of the lien being filed, send notice of the lien that was filed to the Owner and General Contractor.

15th day
Send Intent to Lien letter to General Contractor and Owner.

If at any time during the lien process the project is completed, you must file your lien within 30 days.

TRAP FUNDS

Normally, a lien claimant is only entitled to recover the amount they are owed from retainage. Retainage is 10% of the general contract amount. If there are more lien claimants, then the lien claimants must share the retainage pro rata, meaning it is shared proportionally based on the amount of the lien. The more owed, the higher percentage of retainage the lien claimant is entitled to. However, there is a way to make the owner liable for more than just retainage, called fund trapping. Fund trapping happens when you send notice of your unpaid amount to the owner while they still have more than retainage due to the general contractor. Special language must be included in your notice to invoke fund trapping. The language is listed below and is included in the letter found at **subcontractorinstitute.com**.

If the claim remains unpaid, the owner may be personally liable, and the owner's property may be subjected to a lien unless:

1. *The owner withholds payment from the Contractor for payment of the claim; or*
2. *The claim is otherwise paid or settled.*

Texas Property Code 53.056

It is a good practice to add this language to any notice

letter that you send out. If the owner has more than retainage due to the general contractor when they receive your notice, the owner needs to pay you what you are owed, unless the general contractor disputes the amount you are owed in writing.

If the owner receives your notice, has funds due to the general contractor, and pays the general contractor and not you, the owner will still have to pay your claim even though they have already paid the general contractor. Regardless of the timelines, you can always send the notices early, which will increase the likelihood that you will trap funds in the hands of the owner and get paid faster.

The sooner you send your notice, the more likely you are to trap funds in the hands of the owner and the more likely you are to be paid the full amount you are owed. I saw this play out in real life with a client who was an electrical contractor. It was getting toward the end of their scope and they were owed $60,000. They had not gotten paid for the last two draws they had submitted, and no one was answering the phone at the general contractor's office. They came to my office very concerned about the situation. We started the lien process immediately and sent the first notice to the general contractor and owner with the required fund trapping language. We filed the lien and the client decided to sit on the lien for a little while and not file suit right away. About three weeks later, that client was back in my office: they had been sued. The owner had sued all of the trades that had liens on the project. The lawsuit claimed that although there was over $800,000 in liens against the property, the owner was only responsible for the retainage amount of $300,000, and the lien claimants would have to share that amount. Under that calculation, my client would get less than $30,000 of the $60,000 they were owed.

After we did some discovery, we found that my client had been one of the first lien claimants to send the fund trapping language in a letter to the owner. The owner had paid the general contractor after they had received my client's notice letter. Because the owner had paid the general contractor after they had notice of my client's claims, the owner had to pay my client the full amount they were owed. If the owner pays the general contractor when he knows there are unpaid subcontracts or material suppliers, they will have to pay that same amount again if the contractors and material suppliers remain unpaid.

It is in your best interest to send notice early and often. The earlier you send notice, the more likely you are to be paid in full.

LEASE SPACE

What happens when you are working on a lease space?

Can you file a lien? I see this a lot with restaurants and retail build-outs. Generally speaking, when you are working for a tenant, you can only have a lien against the lease, not the whole property. Why does this matter? When you have a lien on the whole property, you have a lien on the owner's interest in the property. When you have a lien on the lease, you only have a lien on tenants' interest, which does not affect the owner. A lien on the lease has way less leverage than a lien on the whole property.

In some situations, even when you are working for the tenant on the build-out, you can still have a lien on the whole property. If the owner is paying for some or all of the build-out, you may be able to lien the whole property. Payment can be cash or a discount in rent. The problem is that at the time you are doing the work or when it comes time to file a lien, you do not know if the owner is paying for any of the build-out. The only way to know for sure is to see the lease between the owner and the tenant. How do you get that? When the first notice of nonpayment is sent out to the owner, include the following language:

At this time, we are unable to determine if a lien could be filed against just the leasehold interest or the whole property. Please send a copy of the lease with the tenant so the determination can be made regarding which interest the lien will attach. If we do not receive a copy of the lease in the next five days, we will assume the lien will attach to the whole property and file our lien against the whole property.

To determine whether a claimant has a lien on the whole property or just the lease interest, we must be provided with a copy of the lease. If a copy of the lease is not provided within five days, a lien will be filed against the whole property. Send the notice to the owner, the tenant, and the general contractor, if there is one. If you do not receive a copy of the lease or if you receive the lease and it says that the owner is paying for or giving a credit in rent payments for the build-out, file a lien on the whole property. If you find out later that the owner was not really paying for the build-out, you can partly release your lien so it is only against the lease, but you cannot go back later and add the whole property if you only filed your lien against the lease.

WHEN THE LIEN NEEDS TO BE FILED

A lien against a commercial project needs to be filed by the 15th day of the fourth month after you last worked on the project or thirty days after final completion, whichever comes first. This is the same for Place 2, Place 3, and below. You do not have to file a lien for each month you are owed money; as long as you keep sending timely notice of the amounts you are owed for each month you are owed money, you only have to file one lien. If you are owed money for work done in March, April, and May and you sent timely notice of the unpaid amounts, you need to file your lien on or before September 15 or thirty days after final completion, whichever comes first.

NO EXTENSIONS

There is no extension of time to file your lien if the 15th falls on a weekend or holiday. The clerk's office only accepts filings on business days. If you are one day late, your lien will not be valid.

NOTICE OF LIEN

You must send a copy of the lien that you file to the owner and the general contractor within five days of filing the lien. It does not have to be stamped by the county clerk; it just needs to be a copy of what is filed. Like all required notices, it must be sent as certified mail and follow all the requirements we covered in Chapter 3.

PROMISES OF PAYMENT

Never let a promise of payment push you out past the time when you need to send your first notice. Let whoever is making the promise of payment know that you believe them, but that you need to protect your lien rights and have to send the required notices. Normally, if the general contractor has not been paid, they won't mind if you send your notices because it might also be the catalyst that gets them paid.

I know that was a lot of information and steps to follow to have a valid lien, but you can do it. Now, exactly what is required to be in the lien you file is not as rough, and we will go over that in the next chapter.

KEY TAKEAWAYS

- The first notice that needs to be sent on a commercial project for a Place 2 contractor is by the 15th day of the third month.
- The first notice that needs to be sent on a commercial project for a Place 3 contractor is by the 15th day of the second month.
- Make sure you add the language required to trap funds to your notice letter.
- Make sure you ask for a copy of the lease in your notice letter if you are working for a tenant.
- Your lien needs to be filed by the 15th of the fourth month after you last worked or within thirty days of final completion, whichever comes first.
- You need to send out notice of the lien you filed within five days of it being filed.
- Don't let promises of payment push you outside any of these deadlines.

CHAPTER 6

———

THE LIEN FORM

"How was the property sold without first taking care of my lien?" Lily from Super Metalworks Subcontractor asked me. Lily had found a lien form online, filled out what she could, and filed it with the county clerk where the property was located. The lien was missing one key element: the legal description. Without a legal description, the title company was unable to locate Lily's lien because it did not attach to the property. In other words, the lien did not show up on the title commitment and was not taken care of before the property was sold. The lien was therefore unenforceable. A legal description is required to have a valid lien. Lily was unable to recover any money from her lien. This is why it is so important to have your liens filed by a competent attorney.

There is a laundry list of things that must be included

in a lien for it to be valid and enforceable against a property. Missing even one thing can be fatal to a lien's enforceability.

REQUIREMENTS FOR A LIEN

1. **The lien must contain the actual amount that you are owed.** Include the entire amount you are owed. The lien amount should be for the value of work you performed, the materials you supplied that remain unpaid, and retainage. Technically, retainage does not become due until thirty days after final completion, but it does not make sense to file another lien just for retainage. You can always provide a partial release of the lien if you are paid everything but retainage. The amount of the lien can only be for work you have actually done or materials supplied for the project. You cannot lien for your whole contract amount if you did not perform the whole contract. Lien for all amounts you think you are owed, even if it turns out you are actually owed less. Having a lien for more than what you are owed will not invalidate the whole lien, just the portion you are not entitled to. Add in all amounts you are owed when you file the lien, because you cannot amend or edit a lien once it is filed. Each lien must stand or fall on its own, meaning for each lien, you must prove that you sent timely notice and that it was filed on time.

2. **The lien must include the name and last known address of the owner.** We went over how to find this information in Chapter 3.
3. **The lien must include a general statement of the kind of work you did at the property.** This does not have to be anything too specific, just a sentence or two that describes the work you did and the materials you supplied, so the general contractor and owner can figure out who you are.
4. **The lien must include a statement for the months you performed the work for which you are seeking payment.** If you are owed money for work done in June and July, then the lien needs to state that the amount you are claiming is for work done in June and July and retainage.
5. **The lien must include the name and last known address for the general contractor.** If you were not hired by the general contractor, you also need to include the name and last known address of the contractor who hired you.
6. **The lien must include a brief legal description of the property and the county the property is located in.** Although not legally required, it's best to include the address, but the address alone is not enough for a legal description. The appraisal district where the property is located will have a brief legal description in the information provided.
7. **The lien must include your name and address.**

Include both your physical address and your mailing address if they are different.

8. **The lien must include the dates you sent notices to the owner and general contractor and the method by which the notice was sent.**

9. **The lien must be sworn to in front of a notary.** The lien must have a jurat, which means that you are swearing that the information in the lien is true and correct. An acknowledgment is not enough.

10. **If your lien is on a homestead, it needs to include the following heading:** "NOTICE: THIS IS NOT A LIEN. THIS IS ONLY AN AFFIDAVIT CLAIMING A LIEN."

YOU MUST SEND NOTICE OF THE LIEN

To have a valid statutory lien on a homestead, residential, or commercial project, you must send notice of the lien that was filed. This notice must be sent as certified mail just like all the other notices. It must be sent to the owner and general contractor within five days of the lien being filed. If you fail to do this step, your lien will be invalid and unenforceable. You will have no lien rights if you do not send this notice.

A LIEN CANNOT BE AMENDED ONCE IT IS FILED

Once your lien is filed, it cannot be amended. If you

missed something, you will have to file a new lien. The new lien must be timely and meet all the requirements for a valid lien.

FACIALLY VALID

You should be able to tell whether your lien is valid from the information you put in the lien. For your lien to be facially valid, you should be able to tell that all of your notices were sent on time, your lien was filed on time, and your lien has all the required information. You will need to save all of your signed green cards and/ or unclaimed certified letters to prove that everything you state in the lien is true and correct. You do not need to attach invoices, the contract, or your notices to the lien. As long as you have all of the information listed in 1–10 above in your lien and keep all the documents to prove your statements, additional documentation does not have to be filed with the lien.

FACIALLY INVALID

If all of the requirements for a lien cannot be found in the lien that you filed, your lien is invalid and can be removed. If you are missing any of the listed requirements, a motion to remove your lien can be filed. Not only can your lien be removed, but you could have to pay the attorney fees of whoever had to file the motion to remove your lien. If you get a notice that the lien you filed is invalid or fraudulent, don't ignore the notice. Take your lien and the notice you received to a competent attorney and get an opinion on whether your lien is valid. Then you can make the determination if it is worth fighting for or not.

I think it's important to address what can happen if your lien is found to be invalid. I once represented a concrete contractor who had been a client for a while and knew that, although I would use aggressive collections techniques on projects where they had missed their lien timelines, I would not file a lien because it would be invalid. On one project, they were untruthful with me about when their work was performed. They said the work had been done in April, when it had really been done in March. We filed the lien, and in the subsequent litigation, it was clear that the work had been done in March, not in April, which made the lien invalid. Not only did the judge remove my client's lien, but he also issued a judgment that said my client had to pay over $100,000 for the owner's attorney's fees.

The consequences of an invalid lien can be harsh, so make sure you follow the property lien timelines and that everything you put in a lien is truthful and can be verified.

A lien is what is required to have a claim on a privately owned property, but a valid bond claim is what is required to have a claim on property owned by a Texas governmental entity. Even though you cannot file a lien, you can still secure the amount you are owed. Find out how in the next chapter.

KEY TAKEAWAYS

- Lien forms have ten requirements.
- Liens filed in Texas must be facially valid.
- Missing even one of the requirements can make your lien invalid.

CHAPTER 7

HOW TO FILE A VALID BOND CLAIM

WORK DONE FOR A TEXAS GOVERNMENTAL ENTITY

"Say a prayer that we guessed the right bond company," I told Shelby from Super Electrical Subcontractor. Shelby had come to my office on June 14 because she was owed $150,000 for work done on a fire station. The last day she had to file her bond claim was June 15, and Shelby did not have a copy of the bond. Bonds that are required for work done for a Texas governmental entity can only be obtained in two ways: from the general contractor that had to obtain the bond or from the governmental entity having the work done. We called the general contractor that hired Shelby's company and requested a copy of the bond, but they refused to send us a copy. We called the city that was having the fire station built, and they told us to file a public information request to request a copy of the bond. We filed the request, but they have up to thirty days to respond, so we knew we were not going to get a copy of the bond from them in the next twenty-four hours. I had filed bond claims against this general contractor in the past for different clients. Most likely, the general contractor would use the same bond company they had used in the past. From my records, there were two likely bond companies that the general contractor would use. Our only hope was to send the bond claim to both companies and hope that we guessed right. We guessed the right bond company, and the general contractor was in shock because we had figured it out. Shelby got paid everything she was owed the very next week. We were lucky, but you shouldn't leave your right to file a bond claim to luck. Get a copy of the bond before you start working.

You cannot file a lien against a government-owned property, but you can still secure your right to payment in the same way as filing a lien by filing a bond claim.

YOU CANNOT LIEN PROPERTY OWNED BY THE GOVERNMENT

All governmental entities, whether it be the city, county,

or state, have governmental immunity, which means that you can't sue them unless they say you can. The government has not given permission to be sued for unpaid contractors and/or material suppliers on their construction projects. Instead, the law requires the general contractor to have a payment bond to pay all unpaid contractors and material suppliers.

WHAT IS A BOND?

With all this talk about bonds, bond claims, and getting a copy of the bond, I think it is important that we discuss what a bond is. A bond in the physical world is just a few pieces of paper. Below, I have included a copy of a bond I obtained on a project. In the legal world, it is a promise by the insurance company that issued the bond to pay valid bond claimants if the general contractor does not. A bond is not insurance; if a bond company is forced to pay a claim, it will go after the general contractor that obtained the bond for repayment. To obtain a bond, the individual owners or the general contractor must sign a personal guarantee. This means if a bond company is forced to pay a claim, not only will they seek to recover the amounts paid from the general contractor that got the bond, but also from the individual owners. This is why general contractors who obtain bonds try not to give them out unless they have to.

PAYMENT BOND

Travelers Casualty and Surety Company
Hartford, CT 06183

Bond No.: 107272154

CONTRACTOR:
(Name, legal status and address)
Flintco, LLC
2950 North Loop W, Suite 450
Houston, TX 77029

SURETY:
(Name, legal status and principal place of business)
Travelers Casualty and Surety Company
One Tower Square, Hartford, CT 06183

OWNER:
(Name, legal status and address)
Harris County ESD No. 24
20440 Imperial Valley Dr.
Houston, TX 77030

CONSTRUCTION CONTRACT
Date:
Amount: $4,250,000.00 (Four million, two hundred fifth thousand dollars)
Description:
(Name and location)
Harris Count ESD 24 Fire Station #41, 2850 Farrell Road, Houston, TX 77073

BOND
Date:
(Not earlier than Construction Contract Date)
Amount: $4,250,000.00 (Four million, two hundred fifth thousand dollars)
Modifications to this Bond: [x] None   [ ] See Section 18

CONTRACTOR AS PRINCIPAL		**SURETY**	
Company:	*(Corporate Seal)*	Company:	*(Corporate Seal)*
Flintco, LLC		Travelers Casualty and Surety Company	
Signature:		Signature: *Cheryl & m°Aleean*	
Name and Title: Trevor Ladner,		Name and Title: Cheryl L. McAleenan, Attorney-in-Fact	
Authorized Representative			

(Any additional signatures appear on the last page of this Payment Bond.)

(FOR INFORMATION ONLY —Name, address and telephone

AGENT or BROKER:
Hillsdale Insurance Agency
8800 Page Avenue
St. Louis, MO 63114
314-733-2454

§ 1 The Contractor and Surety, jointly and severally, bind themselves, their heirs, executors, administrations, successors and assign to the Owner to pay for labor, materials and equipment furnished for use in the performance of the Construction Contract, which is incorporated herein by reference, subject to the following terms.

§ 2 If the Contractor promptly makes payment of all sums due to Claimants, and defends, indemifies and holds harmless the Owner from claims, demands, liens or suits by any person or entity seeking payment

The Company executing this bond vouches that this document conforms to American Institute of Architects Document A312, 2020 edition for labor, materials or equipment furnished for use in the performance of the Construction Contract, then the Surety and the Contractor shall have no obligation under this Bond.

§ 3 If there is no Owner Default under the Construction Contract, the Surety's obligation to the Owner under this Bond shall arise after the Owner has promptly notified the Contractor and the Surety (at the address described in Section 13) of claims, demands, liens or suits against the Owner or the Owner's property by any person or entity seeking payment for labor, materials or equipment furnished for use in the performance of the Construction Contract and tendered defense of such claims, demands, liens or suits to the Contractor and the Surety.

§ 4 When the Owner has satisfied the conditions in Section 3, the Surety shall promptly and at the Surety's expense defend, indemnify and hold harmless the Owner against a duly tendered claim, demand, lien or suit.

§ 5 The Surety's obligations to a Claimant under this Bond shall arise after the following:

§ 5.1 Claimants, who do not have a direct contract with the Contractor,

    .1 have furnished a written notice of non-payment to the Contractor, stating with substantial accuracy the amount claimed and the name of the party to whom the materials were, or equipment was, furnished or supplied or for whom the labor was done or performed, within ninety (90) dys after having last performed labor or last furnished materials or equipment included in the Claim; and

    .2 have sent a Claim to the Surety (at the address described in Seciton 13).

§ 5.2 Claimants, who are employed by or have a direct contract with the Contractor, have sent a Claim to the Surety (at the address described in Section 13).

§ 6 If a notice of non-payment required by Section 5.1.1 is given by the Owner to the Contractor, that is sufficient to satisfy a Claimant's obligation to furnish a written notice of non-payment under Section 5.1.1.

§ 7 When a Claimant has satisfied the conditions of Sections 5.1 or 5.2, whichever is applicable, the Surety shall promptly and at the Surety's expense take the following actions:

§ 7.1 Send an answer to the Claimant, with a copy to the Owner, within sixty (60) days after the receipt of the Claim, stating the amounts that are undisputed and the basis for challenging any amounts that are disputed; and

§ 7.2 Pay or arrange for payment of any undisputed amounts.

§ 7.3 The Surety's failure to discharge its obligations under Section 7.1 or Section 7.2 shall not be deemed to constitute a waiver of defenses the Surety or Contractor may have or acquire as to a Claim, except as to undisputed amounts for which the Surety and Claimant have reached agreement. If, however, the Surety fails to discharge its obligations under Section 7.1 or Section 7.2, the Surety shall indemnify the Claimant for the reasonable attorney's fees that Claimant incurs thereafter to recover any sums found to be due and owing to the Claimant.

§ 8 The Surety's total obligation shall not exceed the amount of this Bond, plus the amount of reasonable attorney's fees provided under Section 7.3, and the amount of this Bond shall be credited for any payments made in good faith by the Surety.

§ 9 Amounts owed by the Owner to the Contractor under the Construction Contract shall be used for the performance of the Construction Contract and to satisfy claims, if any, under any construction performance bond. By the Contractor furnishing and the Owner accepting this Bond, they agree that all funds earned by the Contractor in the performance of the Construction Contract are dedicated to satisfy

---

The Company executing this bond vouches that this document conforms to American Institute of Architects Document A312, 2020 edition

obligations of the Contractor and Surety under this Bond, subject to the Owner's priority to use the funds for the completion of the work.

§ **10** The Surety shall not be liable to the Owner, Claimants or others for obligations of the Contractor that are unrelated to the Construction Contract. The Owner shall not be liable for the payment of any costs or expenses of any Claimant under this Bond, and shall have under this Bond no obligation to make payments to, or give notice on behalf of, Claimants or otherwise have any obligations to Claimants under this Bond.

§ **11** The Surety hereby waives notice of any change, including changes of time, to the Construction Contract or to related subcontracts, purchase orders and other obligations.

§ **12** No suit or action shall be commenced by a Claimant under this Bond other than in a court of competent jurisdiction in the state in which the project that is the subject of the Constrcution Contract is located or after the expiration of one year from the date (1) on which the Claimant sent a Claim to the Surety pursuant to Section 5.1.2 or 5.2, or (2) on which the last labor or service was performed by anyone or the last materials or equipment were furnished by anyone under the Construction Contract, whichever of (1) or (2) first occurs. If the provisions of this Paragraph are void or prohibited by law, the minimum period of limitation available to sureties as a defense in the jurisdiction of the suit shall be applicable.

§ **13** Notice and Claims to the Surety, the Owner or the Contractor shall be mailed or delivered to the address shown on the page on which their signature appears. Actual receipt of notice or Claims, however accomplished, shall be sufficient compliance as of the date received.

§ **14** When this Bond has been furnished to comply with a statutory or other legal requirement in the location where the construction was to be performed, any provision in this Bond conflicting with said statutory or legal requirement shall be deemed deleted herefrom and provisions conforming to such statutory or other legal requirement shall be deemed incorporated herein. When so furnished, the intent is that this Bond shall be construed as a statutory bond and not as a common law bond.

§ **15** Upon request by any person or entity appearing to be a potential beneficiary of this Bond, the Contractor and Owner shall promptly furnish a copy of this Bond or shall permit a copy to be made.

§ **16 Definitions**
§ **16.1 Claim.** A written statement by the Claimant including at a minimum:
- .1   the name of the Claimant;
- .2   the name of the person for whom the labor was done, or materials or equipment furnished;
- .3   a copy of the agreement or purchase order pursuant to which labor, materials or equipment was furnished for use in the performance of the Construction Contract;
- .4   a brief description of the labor, materials or equipment furnished;
- .5   the date on which the Claimant last performed labor or last furnished materials or equipment for use in teh performance of the Construction Contract;
- .6   the total amount earned by the Claimant for labor, materials or equipment furnished as of the date of the Claim;
- .7   the total amount of previous payments received by the Claimant; and
- .8   the total amount due and unpaid to the Claimant for labor, materials or equipment furnished as of the date of the Claim.

§ **16.2 Claimant.** An individual or entity having a direct contract with the Contractor or with a subcontractor of the Contractor to furnish labor, materials or equipment for use in the performance of the Construction Contract. The term Claimant also includes any individual or entity that has rightfully asserted a claim under an applicable mechanic's lien or similar statute against the real property upon which the Project is located. The intent of this Bond shall be to include without limitation in the terms "labor, materials or equipment" that part of water, gas, power, light, heat, oil, gasoline, telephone service or rental equipment used in the Construction Contract, architectural and engineering services required for performance of the work of the Contractor and the Contractor's subcontractors, and all other items for which a mechanic's lien may be asserted in the jurisdiction where the labor, materials or equipment were furnished.

§ **16.3 Construction Contract.** The agreement between the Owner and Contractor identified on the cover page, including all Contract Documents and all changes made to the agreement and the Contract Documents.

§ **16.4 Owner Default.** Failre of the Owner, which has not been remedied or waived, to pay the Contractor as required under the Construction Contract or to perform and complete or comply with the other material terms of the Construction Contract.

§ **16.5 Contract Documents.** All the documents that comprise the agreement between the Owner and Contractor.

§ **17** If this Bond is issued for an agreement between a Contractor and subcontractor, the term Contractor in this Bond shall be deemed to be Subcontractor and the term Owner shall be deemed to be Contractor.

(Space is provided below for additional signatures of added parties, other than those appearing on the cover page.)

CONTRACTOR AS PRINCIPAL
Company: *(Corporate Seal)*

Signature: _____
Name and Title:
Address:

SURETY
Company: *(Corporate Seal)*

Signature: _____
Name and Title:
Address:

The Company executing this bond vouches that this document conforms to American Institute of Architects Document A312, 2020 edition

TRAVELERS	Travelers Casualty and Surety Company of America Travelers Casualty and Surety Company St. Paul Fire and Marine Insurance Company

POWER OF ATTORNEY

KNOW ALL MEN BY THESE PRESENTS: That Travelers Casualty and Surety Company of America, Travelers Casualty and Surety Company, and St. Paul Fire and Marine Insurance Company are corporations duly organized under the laws of the State of Connecticut (herein collectively called the "Companies"), and that the Companies do hereby make, constitute and appoint **Cheryl. L. McAleenan**, of **St. Louis, Missouri**, their true and lawful Attorney-in-Fact to sign, execute, seal and acknowledge any and all bonds, recongizances, conditional undertakings and other writings obligatory in the nature thereof on behalf of the Companies in their business or guaranteeing the fidelity of persons, guaranteeing the performance of contracts and executing or guaranteeing bond and undertakings required or permitted in any actions or proceedings allowed by law.

IN WITNESS THEREOF, the Companies have cause this instrument to be signed, and their corporate seals to be hereto affixed, this **3rd** day of **February, 2017.**

State of Connecticut

City of Hartford ss.

By: _____
Robert L. Raney, Senior Vice President

On this the **3rd** day of **February, 2017**, before me personally appeared **Robert L. Raney**, who acknowledged himself to the be the Senior Vice President of Travelers Casualty and Surety Company of America, Travelers Casualty and Surety Company, and St. Paul Fire and Marine Insurance Company, and that he, as such, being authorized so to do, executed the foregoing instrument for the purposes therein contained by signing on behalf of the corporations by himself as a duly authorized officer.

In Witness Whereof, I hereunto set my hand and official seal.

My Commission expires the **30th** day of **June, 2021**

_____
Marie C. Tetreault, Notary Public

This Power of Attorney is granted under and by the authority of the following resolutions adopted by the Boards of Directors of Travelers Casualty and Surety Company of America, Travelers Casualty and Surety Company, and St. Paul Fire and Marine Insurance Company, which resolutions are now in full force and effect, reading as follows:

RESOLVED, that the Chairman, the President, any Vice Chairman, any Executive Vice President, any Senior Vice President, any Vice President, any Second Vice President, the Treasurer, any Assistant Treasurer, the Corporate Secretary or any Assistant Secretary may appoint Attorneys-in-Fact and Agents to act for and of behalf of the Company and may give such appointee such authority as his or her certificate of authority may prescribe to sign with the Company's name and seal with the Company's seal bond, recognizances, contracts of indemnity, and other writings obligatory in the nature of a bond, recognizance, or conditional undertaking, and any of said officers of the Board of Directors at any time may remove any such appointee and revoke the power given him or her; and it is,

FURTHER RESOLVED, that the Chairman, the President, any Vice Chairman, any Executive Vice President, any Senior Vice President or any Vice President may delegate all or any part of the foregoing authority to one or more officers or employeees of this Company, provided that each such delegation is in writing and a copy thereof is filed in the office of the Secretary; and it is

FURTHER RESOLVED, that any bond, recognizance, contract of indemnity, or writing obligatory in the nature of a bond, recognizance, or conditional undertaking shall be valid and binding upon the Company when (a) signed by the President, any Vice Chairman, and Executive Vice President, any Senior Vice President or any Vice President, any Second Vice President, the Treasurer, any Assistant Treasurer, the Corporate Secretary or any Assistant Secretary and fuly attested and sealed with the Company's seal by a Secretary or Assistant Secretary; or (b) duly executed (under seal, if required) by one or more Attorneys-in-Fact and Agent pursuant to the power prescribed in his or her certificates of authority or by one or more Company officers pursuant to a writted delegation of authority; and it is

FURTHER RESOLVED, that the signature of each of the following officers: President, any Executive Vice President, any Senior Vice President, any Vice President, any Assisant Vice President, any Secretary, any Assistant Secretary, and the seal of the Company may be affixed by facsimile to any Power of Attorney or to any certificate relating thereto appointing Resident Vice Presidents, Resident Assistant Secretaries or Attorneys-in-Fact for purposes only of executing and attesting bonds and undertaking and other writing obligatory in the nature thereof, and any such Power of Attorney or certificate bearing such facsimile signature or facsimile seal shall be valid and binding upon the Company and any such power so executed and certified by such facsimile signature and facsimile seal shall be valid and binding on the Company in the future with respect to any bond or understanding to which it is attested.

I, **Kevin E. Hughes**, the undersigned, Assistant Secretary of Travelers Casualty and Surety Company of America, Travelers Casualty and Surety Company, and St. Paul Fire and Marine Insurance Company, do hereby certify that the above and foregoing is a true and correct copy of the Power of Attorney executed by said Companies, which remains if full force and effect.

Date this 12ᵗʰ, day of JUNE , 2020

Kevin E. Hughes, Assistant Secretary

To verify the authenticity of the Power of Attorney, please call us at 1-800-421-3880.
Please refer to the above-named Attorney-in-Fact and the details of the bond to
which the power is attached.

STATE OF MISSOURI
COUNTY OF ST. LOUIS

On this 12th day of JUNE , 2020 , before my personally appeared
_____Cheryl L. McAleenan_____, with whom I am personally acquainted, who, being by
me duly sworn, said: That he/she is Attorney-in-Fact of Travelers Casualty and Surety
Company of America, the corporation described in and which executed the foregoing
instrument; that he/she knows the corporate seal of said Company; that said seal
affixed to said instrument is such corporate seal; that it was so affixed by authority of
the Board of Directors thereof and of his/her office under the Standing Resolutions of
said Company; and that he/she signed his/her name thereto as Attorney-in-Fact by like
authority.

Notary Public, Tonya A Meinhardt

NOTARY STAMP

My commission expires: August 15, 2020
Commission #12618776

State of Texas

Claim Notice Endorsement

To be attached to and form a part of Bond No. 107272154.

In accordance with Section 2253.021(f) of the Texas Government Code and
Section 53.202(6) of the Texas Property Code any notice of claim to the named
surety under this bond(s) should be sent to:

**Travelers Casualty and Surety Company of America
One Tower Square
Hartford, Connecticut 06183-6014
(860) 277-0111**

HOW TO GET A COPY OF THE BOND

Generally speaking, there are only two ways to get a copy
of the bond for a Texas public works project. First, the
general contractor gives you a copy of their bond. If you

send the general contractor a written request for a copy of the payment bond, they are required to send you a copy within ten days of the request. But the only penalty for failing to provide a copy is the cost of obtaining a copy of the bond, not your actual claim amount. You can find a draft of this bond request letter at **subcontractorinstitute.com**.

The other way is to send a public information request for a copy of the payment bond to the governmental entity that is having the work done. This is a reasonable option if you have the time. The governmental entity has thirty days to respond to your request for the bond. A draft of a public information request for the bond can be found at **subcontractorinstitute.com**.

BEST PRACTICES

I recommend getting a copy of the general contractor's bond before you sign the subcontract. That way, you have a copy of the bond before any issues arise. The general contractor knows you are informed of your rights right off the bat.

In general, public works projects are slow to pay. If you are not used to public work, make sure you have the cash flow to handle working for at least three or four months without getting paid.

HOW TO PERFECT YOUR BOND CLAIM, PLACE 2 CONTRACTORS

You need to perfect a bond claim in the same way you perfect a lien claim: by sending timely notice. If you are a contractor hired directly by the general contractor (Place 2) your bond claim needs to be sent by the 15th day of the third month after the first month you are owed money for. The Bond claim needs to be sent to the general contractor and the bond company. The bond claim must be sworn and notarized and must include the amount you are currently owed, the amount of any retainage that has not yet become due under the terms of your subcontract with the general contractor, and a statement that all payments and credits have been applied to the amount you are claiming you are owed. You can find a draft of the bond claim letter at **subcontractorinstitute.com**.

Timeline for Valid Texas Bond Claims:
Place 2

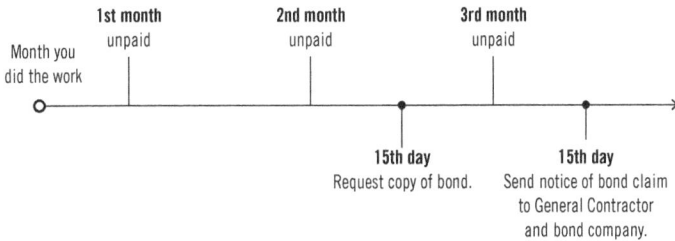

| Month you did the work | 1st month unpaid | 2nd month unpaid | 3rd month unpaid |

15th day
Request copy of bond.

15th day
Send notice of bond claim
to General Contractor
and bond company.

Keep following this process for each month you are owed money.

HOW TO PERFECT YOUR BOND CLAIM, PLACE 3 CONTRACTORS

If you were not hired directly by the general contractor (Place 3 or lower) you can still have a bond claim. You need to send the same notice as required for Place 2 contractors. You also need to send an additional notice the month before you send that notice. On the 15th day of the second month after you are first owed money, you need to send the general contractor notice of your unpaid amounts and any amount of retainage that is not yet due. Just a statement of the amount you are due, what kind of work you did, and who you were hired by is sufficient notice. Find a draft of the second month bond notice letter at **subcontractorinstitute.com**.

Timeline for Valid Texas Bond Claims:
Place 3 and Below

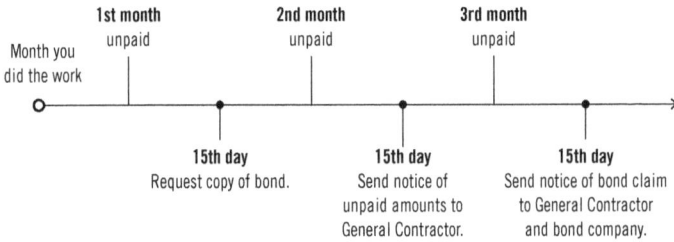

	1st month unpaid	2nd month unpaid	3rd month unpaid
Month you did the work			

	15th day Request copy of bond.	15th day Send notice of unpaid amounts to General Contractor.	15th day Send notice of bond claim to General Contractor and bond company.

Keep following this process for each month you are owed money.

A BOND CLAIM FOR JUST RETAINAGE

A bond claim for just retainage needs to be sent to the general contractor and the bond company on or before the 90th day after completion of the general contractor's contract. A draft of a letter to file your bond claim for retainage can be found at **subcontractorinstitute.com**.

YOU MUST RESPOND TO THE BOND COMPANY'S REQUEST

Once you file your bond claim, you will receive a letter from the bond company requesting your subcontract and all relevant paperwork. You must respond to this letter, or your bond claim will not be paid. It is best to draft a letter explaining how you are owed the amount you are claiming and attach all relevant documents. The bond company will use this information to determine if your claim should be paid or not.

WHEN TO FILE SUIT

Just like a lien claim, you must file suit to enforce your claim, or it will expire. (I will discuss how long liens are good for in Chapter 12.) You must file suit against the bond company to enforce your bond claim within one year of the date you mailed your notice of claim letter. If you do not bring suit within this year, your claim against the bond company will expire and you will only have a claim against the company that hired you. Before you file suit, you must give the bond company and the general contractor sixty days to respond to your bond claim. This gives them time to evaluate your claim and determine if it should be paid before you file your lawsuit.

THE UNBOUND TRUTH ABOUT BOND CLAIMS

Bond claims can be one tough nut to crack, meaning you do not have the same type of leverage with a bond claim that you have with a lien. With a lien, you have leverage with a claim against the owner, pending foreclosure of the lien. With a bond, there is no leverage. If the general contractor or company that obtained the bond does not agree that your claim should be paid, the bond company will not pay. Most bond claims end up in lawsuits to enforce the claim, which means attorney fees and a long legal battle. Price your public works jobs accordingly. If you get in a dispute with the general contractor, it will take a lot of time and attorney fees to get it resolved.

Bond claims at the state level have a lot of ins and outs. Having a valid bond claim on the federal level is easier and straightforward. We will go over bond claims for federal projects in the next chapter.

KEY TAKEAWAYS

- You cannot file a lien against property owned by any state governmental entity.
- You will have to file a bond claim if you are owed money for work done on a project owned by a state government entity.
- A bond is a piece of paper and a promise by an insurance company to pay.
- You need to send notices of the amounts you are owed and a bond claim letter to have a valid bond claim.
- Your bond claim is only good for one year from the date you sent your bond claim letter.
- You must give the general contractor and the bond company sixty days to respond to your claim before you file suit to enforce your bond claim.

___

CHAPTER 8

WHAT CLAIMS DO I HAVE ON A FEDERAL PROJECT?

How can you secure your right to payment if you were hired to do work at an army base or on another federal project?

A FEDERAL BOND

Just like a state bond, a federal bond is just a piece of paper and a promise from an insurance company to pay valid claims if the general contractor does not.

The general contractor on a federal project is required to obtain a payment bond to ensure that Place 2 and Place 3 contractors and material suppliers are paid for the labor and materials they provide. A federal project is any project being paid for by the United States of America. Examples include: airports, army bases, federal prisons, post offices, and more.

Constitutional Food Chain Chart

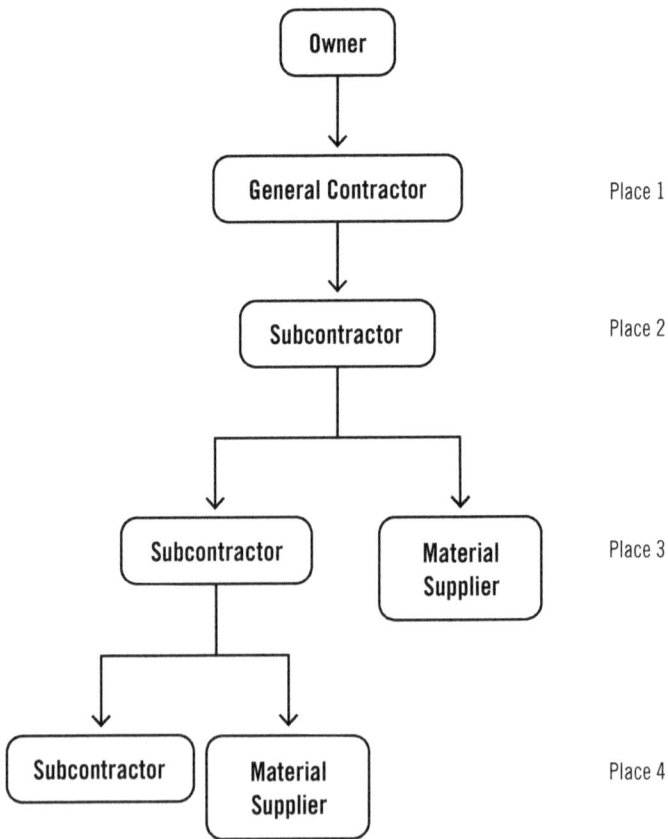

```
                    ┌─────────┐
                    │  Owner  │
                    └────┬────┘
                         ↓
              ┌─────────────────────┐
              │ General Contractor  │        Place 1
              └──────────┬──────────┘
                         ↓
              ┌─────────────────────┐
              │    Subcontractor    │        Place 2
              └──────────┬──────────┘
              ┌──────────┴──────────┐
              ↓                     ↓
     ┌────────────────┐    ┌────────────────┐
     │ Subcontractor  │    │    Material     │   Place 3
     └───────┬────────┘    │    Supplier     │
             │             └────────────────┘
     ┌───────┴───────┐
     ↓               ↓
┌──────────────┐ ┌──────────────┐
│ Subcontractor│ │   Material   │              Place 4
└──────────────┘ │   Supplier   │
                 └──────────────┘
```

Place 4 contractors and material suppliers do not have the right to file a federal bond claim. Just like you cannot file a lien on property owned by a Texas governmental entity, you cannot file a lien on property owned by the federal government.

MAKE SURE THERE IS A BOND BEFORE YOU SIGN THE SUBCONTRACT

The law requires that the general contractor obtain a payment bond for federal projects, but the federal government has no duty to make sure that one is actually provided. Not only that, but the federal government also has no liability to unpaid contractors and material suppliers, even if they have funds due to the general contractor. Let's say the general contractor on an army base project owes your company $100,000 for work done on the project. You request a copy of the general contactor bond from the general contractor and the federal government. You also send notice of your unpaid amounts and notice of claim to the army base. Turns out the general contractor never got a bond, but the federal government still owes the general contractor $500,000. Even though the federal government knows you are owed money, they have no duty to pay you anything and can pay the general contractor the $500,000 without paying you first.

Before you sign a subcontract on a federal project, get

a copy of the general contractor's bond. That way, you know for sure that there is a bond, and you can contact the bond company directly if you are unpaid.

HOW FEDERAL BOND CLAIMS ARE SUPPOSED TO WORK

Here's how federal bond claims are supposed to work: you make a demand for payment from the general contractor, who then forwards that demand to their bond company. There are obvious problems with this system, which is why it is so important to get a copy of the bond before you sign the subcontract. Don't worry if you did not get a copy of the bond before you started working; you can still get a copy, if there is one. You can get a copy from the federal government. To do so, contact your local U.S. General Services Administration. Once you request a copy of a bond for a project, they are required to comply.

WHAT TO DO IF YOU ARE OWED MONEY ON A FEDERAL PROJECT

If you are a Place 2 contractor or material supplier, you need to send the general contractor notice of your bond claim. The notice must be sent within ninety days of last work or last materials supplied. It is not required to be sent to the bond company, but it will give you more leverage if you do so. Therefore, I would recommend sending this notice to the bond company as well. A draft of this notice letter can be found at **subcontractorinstitute.com**. I would also include your outstanding pay applications or invoices.

If you are a Place 2 contractor or material supplier, the only requirement is that you file suit against the bond company within one year after you last worked or supplied materials. If your goal is to get paid faster, send the above notice to the general contractor, bond company, and federal government entity that oversees the project within ninety days of last work or last materials supplied. Although not required, it will get attention and could get you paid without filing a lawsuit.

WHEN A FEDERAL BOND CLAIM EXPIRES

Every place of contractor or material supplier that has filed a bond claim on a federal project has one year after they last worked on the project or last supplied materials to file suit to enforce their bond claim.

SLOW PAY

As a general warning, if you are thinking of venturing into public works projects, either at the state or federal level, make sure you have a decent cash reserve. Payments on public projects are at a government pace, so know going in that it could be a while before you are paid and plan accordingly.

Not getting paid on any project is a pain in the ass, but what would it mean if you could take your stuff back if you were not paid? This type of remedy is not available for bond claims, but it is something to look into for private work in Texas. I will address the gritty details of how you might be able to get your stuff back in the next chapter.

KEY TAKEAWAYS

- You cannot file a lien on a federal project.
- Only Place 2 and 3 contractors and material suppliers can file federal bond claims.
- Get a copy of the general contractor's payment bond before you sign the subcontract.
- If you did not get a copy before you started working, you can get a copy from the federal government, if there is one.
- Send notice of your claim to all parties involved, even if not legally required.
- You have one year after you last worked or supplied materials to file a lawsuit to enforce your claim, or your federal bond claim will expire.
- Make sure you have a decent cash reserve when you start a public project.

CHAPTER 9

___

I DID NOT GET PAID; CAN I TAKE MY STUFF BACK?

"We will be removing all of the light fixtures inside and outside tomorrow at 5 p.m. if my client is not paid in full," I told the owner's attorney. My client was owed $50,000 for the light fixtures they had installed at an event venue. At noon the next day, my client received a cashier's check for the full amount they were owed.

If you have not been paid, you have filed a valid statutory lien, and whatever you installed can be removed without damaging the property, you may have the option of removing your stuff.

USED STUFF, NOT WORTH AS MUCH

Let's be real; we all know that used equipment, appliances, or materials are worth less than new. You won't be made whole by removing what you installed at the project. But look at it from the owner's perspective. What does it do to the property value or the owner's ability to hold events or use the property if what you installed is removed? How can you hold an event without light fixtures? The leverage is in the threat of taking the stuff back, not actually doing it.

YOU MUST HAVE A STATUTORY LIEN

You can take improvements that are "removable," meaning you physically go to the project and take back whatever you have installed. Because this is such a strong remedy, in order to have the right to remove whatever you installed, you must have sent proper notice and have a valid statutory lien. You must have sent timely notice and filed a timely lien. You cannot use the "removable" remedy if you have a constitutional lien.

WHAT IS REMOVABLE?

What is considered "removable" after it is installed? Only those improvements that can be removed without injury to the property or other improvements qualify for this remedy. Some examples of improvements that are removable include: appliances, AC condensers (not ductwork), light fixtures, garbage disposals, carpet, heating components, smoke detectors, burglar alarms, and door locks. This is not an exhaustive list, but here are the things you should consider when trying to make the determination whether what you supplied is removable:

- How is it attached to the property or other improvements? Is it just plugged in, or is it screwed to the wall?
- What would have to be fixed if you removed the item? Is it just installing a new item, or will the wall have to be repainted if it is removed?
- Is the item you are trying to remove 100% installed? For example, was the AC condenser installed and working, or was it just delivered to the property?
- What does the item you want to remove do?

What you are looking for is how much damage the removal of the item will cause. The less damage, the more likely it is that you will be allowed to remove your item.

Some items that have been found to not be removable include: an entire garage building, brick veneer, a fireplace, a chimney, roofing, window frames, paint, and wallpaper. This is not an exhaustive list, but it gives you some idea of what is not considered removable.

DON'T GET ARRESTED

Just because you are allowed to remove some items you have installed does not mean you can break in to get them. If it is something that can be accessed without breaking and entering, you can most likely just go take the item. However, it would be best to consult a competent attorney before you just go taking your stuff back. Removing your items is an extreme remedy, and you want to make sure you do it correctly. You don't want to get sued for removing your items. Even if the owner or general contractor refuses to give you access to the property to remove your items, you can get a court order to allow you to remove your items. So do not just break in and take them.

LEVERAGE

Knowing whether what you installed at the project is removable gives you huge leverage. In most cases, the owner will make sure you get paid before you remove what you installed. The leverage is in the threat of removing the item; it is likely that you will not be made whole by removing what you installed anyway.

Another extreme remedy in the collection world is the ability to file a lien for materials that were not delivered or used at the property. We will discuss what is required to have this type of lien in the next chapter, which covers specially fabricated materials.

KEY TAKEAWAYS

- If you don't get paid and did file a valid statutory lien, you may be able to remove the items you installed if the removal does not damage the property.
- The less damage the removal would cause, the more likely you will be able to remove your stuff.
- Get the opinion of a competent attorney before you begin the removal process.
- Do not break the law to remove your stuff.
- The leverage with removable items is the threat of the removal; rarely will you be made whole by taking your stuff.

CHAPTER 10

SPECIALLY FABRICATED MATERIALS

"What am I supposed to do with $40,000 worth of the wrong color stone?" Holly from Super Masonry Subcontractor (SMS) asked me. SMS had been hired on a large hotel project. They had submitted samples of the stone, which the general contractor had approved. The stone that was approved was special order and had a six-week lead time. Holly ordered the stone, and it was ready to be delivered to the project site. Now the owner wanted a different type of stone. Holly had to pay her material supplier for the stone, but now what was she going to do? Holly came to see me just in time. We were able to file a lien for the stone even though it was never delivered to the property. The owner paid Holly in full for the $40,000.

You can file a lien for specially fabricated materials even if they are never delivered or installed at the project site.

WHAT ARE SPECIALLY FABRICATED MATERIALS?

Specially fabricated materials are materials that are made specifically for that project and cannot really be used anywhere else. Paint that has been tinted for a specific project qualifies as a specially fabricated material. Although the paint could be used somewhere else, it was made for a specific project, so it qualifies as specially fabricated materials. Some other materials that would qualify as specially fabricated include but are not limited to: carpet, custom windows, tinted finish, tile, and wallpaper.

NOTICE FOR SPECIALLY FABRICATED MATERIALS

If you remain unpaid for specially fabricated materials that are not delivered or used at the project, you can file a lien for such materials. The notices that must be sent to have a lien for such materials are slightly different than the notices required for materials that are delivered. Furthermore, such notice needs to be sent sooner.

If you need to file a lien for undelivered specially fabricated materials, you must send notice of the amount you are owed no later than the 15th day of the second month after you receive and accept the order of the specially fabricated materials. For example, if Holly placed the order with her material supplier in June and they accept the order in June, she needs to send notice of the unpaid amounts for the specially fabricated materials on or before August 15.

The notice that must be sent by the 15th day of the second month must go to the owner and the general contractor. The notice must contain:

1. A statement that the specially fabricated materials have been ordered, received, and accepted, and
2. The price of the order.

A draft of notice can be found at **subcontractorinstitute. com**. If the specially fabricated materials are delivered to the project site, the normal timelines apply.

Of course, the notice must be sent as certified mail, return receipt requested, and as I have mentioned before, the only way to prove when a letter was sent is to take it to the post office and have it stamped.

FILING THE LIEN

The timeline for filing the lien still remains the same. For commercial projects, it is the 15th day of the fourth month after you last worked; for a residential project, it is the 15th day of the third month. Or, for both commercial and residential projects, within thirty days of final completion, whichever comes first. Please note you must send timely notice to have a valid lien.

WHAT SHOULD YOU DO WITH THE SPECIALLY FABRICATED MATERIALS?

First, you should try to deliver the materials to the project site. Then they will no longer be your issue. If the materials are refused and they are either sitting at your office or your material supplier's warehouse, what should you do? Send a letter to the general contractor and the owner explaining the full situation, that you plan to sell the materials for a reduced amount, and that any amount received will be subtracted from the amount owed. Because they refused delivery, they have no right to object to the amount received for the materials, and you can still expect to be paid the full amount owed. You can find a draft of this letter at **subcontractorinstitute.com**.

If you can sell the materials for less than what is owed, sell the materials and apply any amount you received toward what you are claiming is owed. At this point, you can decide if you want to move forward with foreclosure of the lien, or you can just sit.

What do you do if you are paid, but the party that paid for the materials does not want the materials? You send a letter to the general contractor, owner, and party that paid for the materials (if not the owner and/or general contractor), stating that the materials have been paid for and now they need to be picked up or delivered. If no one contacts you within thirty days, you can get rid of the materials however you want. You can find a draft of this letter at **subcontractorinstitute.com**.

Another situation where a lien may be necessary to collect the amounts you are owed is retainage. In the next chapter, I will tell you how to collect your retainage 100% of the time.

KEY TAKEAWAYS

- You can file a lien for specially fabricated materials even if they are not delivered or used at the property.
- The timeline to send notice is shorter than the normal lien timeline, and the notice contains some additional language.
- You can sell the specially fabricated materials for less than what they cost if they are not wanted and you send notice.

CHAPTER 11

HOW TO COLLECT RETAINAGE EVERY TIME

Do you know your profit margin on your projects? Is it more than 10%? You are a real badass if you make a 10% margin on your projects; keep up the good work! But for most contractors, 10% is most of, if not all of, their profit on a project. So tell me, why do so many contractors just walk away from retainage? Retainage is where the profit is. Don't you want to make a profit?

Don't just walk away from your profit. Follow the steps in this chapter, and you will collect your retainage.

WHAT IS RETAINAGE?

Legally speaking, retainage is 10% of the contract amount between the owner and general contractor. There is no legal requirement that retainage be withheld from a contractor. The owner withholds the 10% from the general contractor, and the general contractor retains the 10% from all of its subs so they do not have to pay the 10% out of pocket.

WHY RETAINAGE IS IMPORTANT

Retainage can limit the owner's liability to lien claimants in two ways. First, retainage can limit the amount the owner is required to pay lien claimants. If the owner properly withholds the 10% from the general contractor, the 10% is the only liability they will have to lien claimants. This means that if the total of all the amounts due to lien claimants is more than retainage, the lien claimants will have to share the retainage pro rata. The owner will not have to pay them all in full. Instead, their only liability is the amount of retainage. The other way the owner can limit their liability to lien claimants is by shortening the deadline to file a lien. Normally, a lien claimant has until the 15th of the third or fourth month, depending on the type of project, after they last supplied labor or materials to file their lien. If the owner properly withholds retainage from the general contractor, the timeframe for lien claimants to file their liens is shortened to thirty days after final completion regardless of when they performed their work or supplied materials. Which is why your lien always needs to be filed within thirty days of final completion regardless of where you are in the normal lien process.

WHEN DOES RETAINAGE BECOME DUE?

Retainage becomes due to the general contractor thirty days after final completion. Generally, what is in subcontracts is that retainage becomes due to the contractor when the general contractor is paid retainage. If the general contractor is not getting paid retainage until thirty days after final completion, there is no way you are getting paid retainage before the timeframe for filing your lien runs out. If the owner withholds the retainage, all liens must be filed within thirty days of final completion.

FILE A LIEN TO MAKE SURE TO COLLECT RETAINAGE

It is so common for contractors to come to me five or six months after a project is completed saying they have not been paid retainage and asking how I can help them collect their money. At this point, it is way too late to file a lien. The only option they have it to sue the general contractor or whoever hired them for breach of contract. That is time-consuming and expensive; a lien against the project is way more efficient. The owner will make sure you are paid out of the general contractor's retainage or ensure that the general contractor pays you.

To be paid retainage in a timely manner, or even at all, you need to file a lien. Include the cost of filing a lien into your project cost and plan on filing a lien to collect your retainage. If you don't file a lien, that means the general contractor may pay your retainage once they are paid retainage, but they will do that on their own timeframe or, in most cases, not at all. Secure your right to timely payment of your retainage and file a lien.

IDENTIFY THAT YOUR LIEN IS FOR RETAINAGE

As long as your lien is filed before thirty days after final completion (assuming you complied with all other rules), it will be timely. However, when you file your lien, make sure you clearly label that it is only for retainage. That way, if you file your lien before the end of the project, the owner can see it is for retainage and not withhold progress draws from the general contractor, and they will make sure you are paid before the final payment to the general contractor.

I HAVE NOT BEEN PAID RETAINAGE—DO I HAVE TO HONOR A WARRANTY CLAIM?

I get phone calls from clients all of the time asking this

question. Unfortunately, it's after they have done the work and have not been paid retainage that the owner is making a warranty claim. All I can say is, "What does your contract or the warranty you issued say?" Then, 90% of the time, the subcontract says they have to do the warranty work even if they have not been paid retainage. How do you fix this issue? Negotiate the subcontract to say that you will not honor warranty claims until you have been paid retainage. An alternative option is that when you issue your warranty paperwork, you make sure it states that you will not honor any claims until you have been paid in full, including retainage.

DO NOT WALK AWAY FROM YOUR PROFIT

Most, if not all, of your profit for your project is in the retainage payment. Don't just walk away from retainage! I hear all the time, "If I file a lien, this general contractor will never hire me again." If it is going to cost you money to have a customer, they are not worth having. If you don't make a profit on a project, that means you did not make money. Even worse, if you lost money on a project, that means you paid to work for the general contractor. How long do you think you can stay in business if you are paying the general contractor to go to work every day and do not make a profit?

Collecting your money is essential to any successful business. The faster you collect it, the better. Ending up in protracted litigation to collect your money is never a win. That is why the next chapter will review the best strategies for collecting your money when a lien has been filed.

KEY TAKEAWAYS

- To get paid retainage, you will need to file a lien. Figure the cost of filing a lien into your project cost.
- Label your lien as a claim for your retainage.
- You are walking away from your profit if you do not collect your retainage.

CHAPTER 12

HOW TO ENFORCE YOUR LIEN

I have successfully collected thousands of liens. The technical remedy for a lien is foreclosure and sale of the property that the lien is filed against. In the few occasions that I have had clients that wanted to purchase the property their lien was filed against at the foreclosure sale, it was a nightmare. For example, I represented a client that foreclosed their $10,000 lien against a property that was valued in excess of $350,000. When the property was posted for sale, my client was the highest bidder and purchased the property for $10,000. The owner of the property had been sent all of the required notices, and everything was done legally. The owner had ignored everything until we went to change the locks on the doors. All of a sudden, the owner paid attention and thought it was unfair that we could take his $350,000 property for $10,000 and filed suit against my client. Although we had done everything correctly, it took three years of litigation to come to the resolution of selling the property and splitting the proceeds.

Although foreclosure of the property is the ultimate remedy for an unpaid lien, the best result is getting paid your lien amount and any attorney fees you have incurred. The idea that you could just end up with the property is too good to be true.

HOW LONG ARE LIENS GOOD FOR?

How long your lien is good for depends on the type of property your lien is filed against. If your lien is against a commercial property, you have two years after the last day you could have filed your lien to file a lawsuit to foreclose your lien before it expires. A good rule of thumb that I tell my clients is you have two years from the date your lien was filed to file a lawsuit to enforce your lien. If your lien is on a residential property, you have one year after the last day you could have filed your lien to file a lawsuit to foreclose your lien before it expires. I use the same rule of thumb for residential properties: you have one year after your lien is filed to file a lawsuit to enforce your lien.

If your lien expires, you are no longer entitled to enforce your lien, and if the owner and/or general contractor demands a release of your expired lien, you need to provide one. If you don't release your expired lien, you could be sued for removal of the lien and have to pay someone's attorney fees that were incurred in removing your lien. It is always a good idea to get the opinion of a competent attorney to determine whether your lien has expired.

SHOULD I STAY OR SHOULD I GO NOW?

The question I always get when I file a lien for my clients is "What happens now?" What happens after the lien is filed depends on the particular case, but I will tell you all the things that you need to consider before choosing a course of action once your lien is filed.

IS THERE A BANK INVOLVED?

The first and probably the most important thing to consider is this: is there a bank involved in paying for the construction? This matters for several reasons. Most construction projects that have a bank involved are in construction financing while the project is being built. While the loan is in construction financing, the owner is only paying interest on the loan and not anything toward the principle. Once the construction project is finished, the loan will go from construction financing to permanent financing. When this happens, there is another closing, and all liens that are filed need to be taken care of before this closing. What does this mean for you? If you have filed a lien on a project that is in construction financing, you may want to consider sitting on your lien for a while (not foreclosing) because the owner will have to deal with your lien before they go to permanent financing. When you sit on your lien, you just wait. You don't file suit.

Even if you filed a lien against a project that is already in permanent financing, you still have some additional leverage. Banks as a general rule do not like liens on properties they have loans on. Technically, the owner is in default under their loan agreement with the bank by having a lien filed against the property. If your lien is filed against property that has financing, it is worth a call to the bank to let them know about your lien. Some banks will get involved and make sure your lien is taken care of, but some banks don't care. To find out if a property is under financing, you can research the real property records or hire an attorney to do the research and call the bank on your behalf. In this situation, if the bank does not care whether its loans carry liens, your best option is to file suit to foreclose your lien.

WILL THE PROPERTY SELL SOON?

The second thing that should be considered when making

the determination whether to sit on your lien or to file suit is if the property will sell in the near future. If a sale is happening or likely to happen, you don't need to file suit to foreclose your lien. Your lien will have to be dealt with before the property can be sold.

Notice that in both situations, I said that your lien would have to be dealt with, not that it would have to be paid. Your lien can either be paid or bonded. I discuss bonding in more detail in Chapter 14.

SHOULD YOU FILE SUIT?

If the property is neither in construction financing nor likely to be sold in the near future and you don't want to wait for something to happen, you should file suit to foreclose your lien. When I represent clients that have done repair work to existing apartment complexes, I normally recommend that they file suit to foreclose their liens. This is because existing apartment complexes generally are in permanent financing and are not sold very often. If you do not file suit, your lien will not affect the apartment complex.

WHAT HAPPENS WHEN YOU FORECLOSE YOUR LIEN?

Filing a lawsuit to foreclose your lien sounds dramatic, but it is really not exciting. What happens is that a lawsuit is filed against the owner, which basically says, "I have followed all of the rules to have a valid lien; pay me now, or we will move forward and get a court order foreclosing the lien." This gets the attention of the owner, since no one wants to be sued and have to hire an attorney to defend themselves. Most of the time, an owner being served with the lawsuit is enough to get your lien paid. If not, it will be a longer process, which all depends on the facts of your case.

IT'S EASY TO RAISE A FACT QUESTION

If you are a contractor, the owner and general contractor will have an easier time of raising fact questions as to the amount that you are entitled to recover on your lien than if you were a material supplier. A fact question is a statement by the owner or general contractor that questions the amount you are due. It's an expensive process to overcome a fact question in a courtroom.

I once had a client who was owed $5,000 on a residential project. A company owned the property and was building a house to sell. Our plan was to file the lien and then wait for the sale and get paid out of closing. Instead, the owner sued my client, claiming defective work. There had been no claims of defective work until the lawsuit was filed. However, just by saying there was defective work, the owner ensured that there was no fast way out of the case, and we had to go to trial. I tried to get my client to settle, but both sides were dug in. The owner took the position that he was not going to be bullied by some small-time contractor, and my client took the position that he was not just going to roll over and definitely was not going to pay the owner to get out of the case, which was what the owner was demanding to settle the dispute.

To gather all the evidence required to defeat the claims of bad work and prepare for trial cost $60,000. Although we were the defendant (the party that had been sued), we won because we were successful in showing the court that there was nothing defective with my client's work. But the judge thought it was ridiculous that the parties could not have settled this case sooner and only gave my client the $5,000 and $40,000 of his attorney fees. He was still $20,000 short of being made whole financially, not to mention all the time he had to spend on this case in depositions, going through the evidence, getting ready for trial, and attending the trial, which added up to hundreds of hours gone.

So before you head to the courtroom, know that the best you could possibly hope for is to break even—and that rarely happens. You have a better chance taking all the money you would pay an attorney to litigate to the casino. Make sure you are aware of all the risks of the courtroom before you head in that direction.

That is why, in the next chapter, we will get into the most common defenses that are brought up once a lawsuit to foreclose a lien is filed. If you know in advance what defenses will be brought up, you can better prepare while the project is ongoing.

KEY TAKEAWAYS

- A good rule of thumb is that commercial liens are good for two years after they are filed and residential liens are good for one year from the date they're filed.
- Determining whether you should file a lawsuit to enforce your lien after it is filed is something that needs to be determined on a case-by-case basis.

CHAPTER 13

———

COMMON DEFENSES TO LIENS

"What do you mean they are saying my work is bad and has to be redone? The whole time I was at the project, they kept telling me how great the paint looked! How can they now say it was not done correctly?" Chase from Super Painting Subcontractor asked me. It is not uncommon for general contractors or owners to suddenly claim bad work when they receive a notice of lien. In the long run, their claim of bad work won't succeed, but it is effective in slowing down the lien foreclosure process. Super Painting Subcontractor did end up collecting the money they were owed, but it took six months and a lot of attorney fees.

When you file a lien or threaten to file a lien, it is not

uncommon for issues you have never heard of to arise. We will go over the most common defenses to liens and how to prepare for them while you are on the project.

CLAIMS OF BAD WORK

One of the most common defenses to a contractor's liens are claims of bad or defective work. What I normally see happen is we send out a notice of an intent to lien and, in response, we receive a letter stating the work was subpar. This is the first time the contractor has heard that there is any issue with the work. At the end of the day, it will be hard for the general contractor or owner to prove that the work was really defective if there was nothing in writing about the defective work before the lien process began. But what it can do is slow down the process of getting you paid. You can't just go into court and say "Look, judge, I followed all of the rules, so give me a judgment where I win." Instead, you will have to go through a long and expensive litigation process to prove what you are owed.

HOW TO LIMIT THE EFFECT OF BOGUS BAD WORK CLAIMS

Some things you can do while you are on the project to limit the effects of a bogus bad work claim include: submittals, daily reports, and submitting your as-built drawings as soon as you are done with a transmittal letter.

In my first book, *Quit Getting Screwed*, there is a chapter that goes in depth into each of these concepts. The main thing to note is that these are all ways to tell the story of the project while it is happening—what we refer to as CYA (cover your ass). If there is no response indicating defective work as you are submitting these documents throughout the project, it will be difficult for a bad work claim to be used against you later.

THE TIMING OF YOUR WORK

Since the month your work was performed is essential for a valid lien, another common defense to a contractor lien is for the owner or general contractor to claim that you performed your work earlier than what you put on your invoices or state in your lien. If the general contractor or owner can prove that your work was done earlier than you say it was, your lien or a portion of your lien will be invalid. Not only will you not be able to recover the amount you are owed, but you would also be responsible for any attorney fees incurred to remove your lien or any portion of your lien.

Remember, it is not the date of your invoice that matters. It is the date you performed the actual work or supplied the materials. Things you can do while you are on the project to corroborate when the work was performed include: daily reports with pictures, accurate and detailed time records, and approved pay applications. Keeping in mind that when you performed your work could be an issue later on will help you be more conscious about what you put in your daily reports, time records, and pay applications. Remember that whatever day the work was done or materials supplied—whether it was the 1st, 30th, or 31st of the month—it counts as being done in that month. It does not matter what you put on your invoice.

THOSE MATERIALS DID NOT GO HERE

Another defense that commonly arises in response to a lien is that the materials you are claiming payment for were not used at the project. This is a more common defense in the case of material suppliers, but it is a defense that contractors should be aware of as well.

Even if you do not get paid by the general contractor or owner, you still have the obligation to pay your material supplier. If your material supplier takes steps to perfect its lien, it is in your best interest that they are paid, because it is one less bill you will have to pay. What steps can you take to make sure there is ample proof the materials were delivered and used at the project? First, make sure you sign the material suppliers' delivery tickets when the materials are supplied to the project. Second, if your material supplier needs your help to prove that the materials were used at the project, help them out. Don't dodge their calls! If you have not been paid for your work, they will understand, and they still need your help to get paid. You can sign an affidavit that states that all the materials were delivered and used at the property. **Subcontractorinstitute.com** has a draft of a form that you can use.

Also add the delivery of materials to your daily report. Regardless of whether you bring materials or they are delivered to the project site, having the delivery ticket attached to the daily report will go miles in proving the materials were delivered and used at the project.

Another way a general contractor or owner can reduce the effectiveness of your lien is by bonding a private project or bonding around your lien. This is what we will discuss in the next chapter.

KEY TAKEAWAYS

- The common defenses to liens are: your work was defective, you did your work earlier than you said you did, and the materials you are claiming payment for were not used at this project.
- Daily reports, submittals, as-built drawings, signed delivery tickets, and affidavits stating that all the materials were used at the project can make the defenses to liens less effective.

CHAPTER 14

BONDS ON PRIVATE PROJECTS

"What does that mean, they bonded around my lien?" Jessica from Super Plumbing Subcontractor (SPS) asked me. I answered, "It means they can move forward with selling the property without paying your lien."

Jessica had hired my firm to file a lien for the $100,000 her company was owed for work done on a new shopping center. Since the project was in construction financing, I suggested that Jessica wait a little while before she filed suit to foreclose her lien. She had received a notice of bond in the mail and came to me to find out what it meant. "You still have your lien, but now we have to sue the bond company that issued the bond instead of the owner," I explained.

With the leverage of SPS's lien being greatly reduced because the bond eliminated the urgency of having to deal with the lien, the litigation process ensued. After a year in litigation, Jessica accepted $75,000 total to settle the claim because the cost of the attorney fees to keep litigating was killing her company. Not only did Jessica give up $25,000 of her company's lien amount, but she also was not reimbursed any of her $20,000 in attorney fees.

Bonds on private property are available and will reduce the amount of leverage your lien can have. There are two different types of private work bonds.

BOND TO PAY LIENS OR CLAIMS

A bond to pay liens or claims works as an umbrella to protect the owner from lawsuits from lien claimants. This type of bond is issued in the full contract amount and will be available to satisfy all valid lien claims if the general contractor does not pay them.

Generally, these types of bonds are required by the owner on large commercial projects. The owner makes the general contractor obtain this type of bond to protect itself and the property from any lien claims. This type of bond is required to be filed of record with the county clerk where the property is located. The bond must be in the full amount of the general contract and must have a copy of the contract or a memorandum attached.

How does this type of bond affect your lien rights? First, in order to have a valid lien, you need to send your notices to the bond company, as well as all the other required parties. Second, your lien does lose some of its effectiveness because the property and the owner are protected from the effect of your lien. Most likely, you will have to file a lawsuit to enforce your lien to get paid. The good thing about this type of bond is that even if the owner and the general contractor go bankrupt, you will still get paid by the bond company.

BOND TO INDEMNIFY AGAINST LIEN

This type of bond is filed after you filed your lien. This is what is referred to as "bonding around" your lien. That is why when I think of this type of bond, I imagine that the bond puts your lien in a bubble. When you file a lien, it attaches to the property. When a bond to indemnify is filed, a bubble is placed around your lien; your lien is still there, but it no longer attaches to the property. This means that the owner can move forward with any sale or refinancing without having to deal with your lien.

In order for the bond to be an effective bubble around your lien, there are several requirements:

1. The bond must be filed of record with the county clerk in the same county where the lien has been filed.
2. The bond must describe the property the lien is filed against.
3. The bond must refer by the clerk's file number to the lien being bonded.
4. The bond amount must be double the lien amount or, if the lien is over $40,000, be 1.5 times the lien amount or the lien amount plus $40,000, whichever is greater.
5. The bond needs to be payable to the party that filed the lien.
6. The bond must be issued by an authorized surety.
7. Notice and a copy of the bond must be sent as certified mail to the lien claimant.
8. Proof that the notice was sent to the lien claimant must be filed in the real property records.

If these requirements are not followed, the bond will not be effective, meaning there is no bubble around your lien and it still attaches to the property. If this is the case, you can file suit against the owner to enforce your lien.

Your process to have a valid lien is still the same. What is required to enforce your lien changes. Now, instead of filing suit against the owner to enforce your lien, you will have to file suit against the bond company.

LIFE OF LIEN SHORTENED

If a bond to pay liens or claims is recorded at the time you file your lien, you only have one year from the time you file your lien to file suit to enforce your lien or it will expire. Normally, on commercial projects, your lien is valid for two years, but this is shortened to one year if this type of bond is filed. If the bond is not on file when you file your lien but is filed after, you have two years to file suit against the bond company to enforce your lien. This means that if you received a notice that your lien has been bonded around, you will need to file suit if you want to get paid. Once you received the bond notice, take all your paperwork to a qualified attorney and get an opinion and a plan on the best way to proceed. Another tactic that can be used to reduce the effectiveness of your lien and your lien rights are lien waivers. Signing the wrong waiver at the wrong time could forfeit all of your lien rights. Find out which ones to sign and when in the next chapter.

KEY TAKEAWAYS

- There are two different types of bonds for private projects: bonds to pay liens or claims and bonds to indemnify against liens.
- Both types of bonds protect the owner and the property, so your lien loses some of its leverage.
- If the bond to pay liens or claims has been filed before

your lien is filed, you need to send the bond company and all other required parties notice of your claim and lien to have a valid lien.

- Both types of bonds can reduce the amount of time your lien is valid.

CHAPTER 15

―――

LIEN WAIVERS AND LIEN RELEASES

Would you lie if someone asked you to? Well, that is what you are doing if you sign an unconditional lien waiver if you have not been paid. Not only that—you are swearing in front of a notary that what you are saying is true. Based on personal experience, once you say it in writing sworn in front of a notary, it is nearly impossible to take back that statement.

I once represented Super Equipment Rental Subcontractor (SERS) to collect money they were owned on a large commercial project. We sent the third month required notice to the owner and general contractor for amounts owed for equipment rented in the months of April, May, and June; the total amount they were due was $80,000.

In response to the notice, I received a copy of an unconditional lien waiver SERS had signed. The unconditional lien waiver stated that SERS had been paid in full (though it was only $40,000) for the time period ending June 30. In other words, my client had signed an unconditional lien waiver yielding their right to the payment of the additional $40,000. Because the unconditional lien waiver stated they had been paid in full through June 30, I could not file a lien, and SERS was not paid the remaining $40,000 they were owed.

LIEN WAIVERS

The state of Texas has made the lien waiver form standard. If you need a copy of the state form, you can find it at **subcontractorinstitute.com**. There are four standard forms:

1. Conditional upon progress payment
2. Unconditional upon progress payment
3. Conditional upon final payment
4. Unconditional upon final payment

When you submit your first pay application, you include a conditional upon progress payment lien waiver that states the amount you are owed for that time period, not including any amounts owed for retainage. So, you will fill out the lien waiver with the amount of money you are requesting. For the next pay application, you fill out the same conditional lien upon progress payment lien waiver for the time you are requesting payment. You will also include an unconditional upon progress payment lien waiver for the time period for the first pay application if you have been paid and the check has cleared the bank. You will keep submitting lien waivers in this pattern until the final pay application.

For the final pay application, you submit a conditional upon final payment lien waiver, which includes all amounts you are owed, including retainage. Once you are paid everything, including retainage, and the check has cleared the bank, you will issue a unconditional lien waiver upon final payment.

DANGERS OF SIGNING AN UNCONDITIONAL LIEN WAIVER WHEN YOU HAVE NOT BEEN PAID

Both of the unconditional lien waivers have the following warning on the top of the document:

NOTICE:

This document waives rights unconditionally and states that you have been paid for giving up those rights. It is prohibited for a person to require you to sign this document if you have not been paid the payment amount set forth below. If you have not been paid, use a conditional release form.

Attempting to argue that you have not been paid when you signed a document with this warning on top is nearly impossible. What I normally see happen is the general contractor or owner demand that the contractor sign an unconditional lien waiver for promise of a check, but the check never comes. If that happens, there is nothing to be done. The contractor's right to collection has been waived. You have now been warned of the risk of signing an unconditional lien waiver if you have not been paid. You can make the best decision for your business.

LIEN WAIVER VERSUS LIEN RELEASE

The process described above is when and how lien waivers are used. A lien release only needs to be issued if you have actually filed a lien with the county clerk. A lien release form can be found at **subcontractorinstitute. com**. An effective lien release must have the correct legal description of the property and reference by file number the lien that is being released.

Once your lien has been paid, you must issue a lien release within ten days of payment. You do not have an obligation to record the release with the county clerk. It is always a good idea to send the original release as certified mail so you can prove that you sent the release and on what date it was sent. The release must be notarized, and only the original release can be recorded.

Having a clear understanding of the way lien waivers work before you start a project is essential. It is also essential to have a clear and consistent collection strategy for your company. I will go over what you need to know to do this in the next chapter.

KEY TAKEAWAYS

- In Texas, there are standard lien waiver forms to be used during a construction project.
- Don't sign an unconditional lien waiver if you have not been paid in full.
- A lien release only needs to be used if you have filed a lien with the county clerk.
- If you have been paid, you need to issue a lien release within ten days of payment.

CHAPTER 16

HOW TO CREATE A CONSISTENT COLLECTION STRATEGY

A common misconception among all businesses—not just those in the construction industry—is that collections begins when you are owed money. That should not be the case. Collection starts before you decide to extend credit. Before you provide work or materials on credit, there is some thought put into the fact that there may be collection issues in the future. Being intentional about the fact that, at any time, this new favorite customer could become a collection issue continues throughout the business relationship.

WHAT INFORMATION YOU NEED BEFORE YOU START THE PROJECT

Always have a copy of the signed contract in you records before you start working. Don't wait on a promise that they will get the contract back to you later. Insist that you have a copy of the signed contract before you begin working.

Do the research and know who the owner is and have their correct address before you begin the project. This will ensure that, if an issue does arise, you are ready to go. It is also good to do a little extra research to see if you can find a phone number for the owner. A phone call to the owner letting them know you have not been paid can be very effective. Regardless of the outcome of any phone conversations or promises, make sure you follow the correct lien requirements until you receive actual payment.

Make sure you have the correct address and phone number for the general contractor, and specifically whom you need to speak to about your payments, so you are not trying to figure it out when you are owed money.

Find a good attorney and know how much they will charge you for a lien. This is so very valuable. Trying to make a hard lien deadline and find a competent attorney who is familiar with liens can be very stressful, and you may not get it done on time and miss the deadline. Trust me, it is a breath of fresh air when you have an attorney that you work with and all you have to do is pick up the phone and say, "I have an issue," and they handle everything from there.

Another way to push things along if you have an attorney that you work with is to send an email to the general contractor and the owner and cc your attorney. This way, your attorney does not have to do anything, so you won't get a bill, but it is made clear that you have an attorney that has got your back if the issues are not resolved.

SALES VERSUS COLLECTIONS

One of the first lessons I learned as a small business owner is that you cannot effectively be the salesperson and the bill collector; it just does not work. If the salesperson and the collection department are the same person, your customer will not answer the phone if they owe you money or think that you are calling to collect a bill. Even if it is someone else that works for your company, let them be the bad cop and make the collection efforts.

KEEP ACCURATE RECORDS AND REVIEW THEM EVERY MONTH

The key to a successful strategy is knowing when you

are owed money and how much you are owed. Honestly, the only way you can truly keep accurate records is to have some type of accounting software and use it properly. There are a lot of options out there; I personally use QuickBooks, which is a great way to organize your financial information and is super easy to give to your accountant come tax time. Input every invoice and pay application into your accounting system, and at the end of every month, pull a report that shows you all of your outstanding invoices. With that information at hand, you can decide which files need action to protect your rights.

MAKE SURE YOU KNOW AND FOLLOW YOUR LIEN TIMELINES

Knowing and following your lien timelines is essential for a profitable business. Without a lien, your likelihood of collecting your money is around 50%, but with a lien, it's more like 95%. As I explained in Chapter 1, a lien gives you security.

STAND UP FOR YOURSELF AND QUIT GETTING SCREWED

Quit being afraid to take action! The money you are owed represents your labor, effort, and time away from your family. You should fight for it. If you can't do it for yourself, do it so the people that work for you can have a job and feed their families. They are relying on you to do the right thing.

KEY TAKEAWAYS

- Have a collection strategy before you extend credit to anyone.
- Collect all the valuable information you need to know about the project before you begin working.
- Separate your sales and collections departments.
- Know your lien timelines and always follow them.
- Stand up for your company and collect the money you are owed.

CONCLUSION

You now have the required information to run an unstoppable business. Applied knowledge is power. Imagine all of the business opportunities that open up when you can secure the money you are owed. That's what knowing what a lien is and what your lien rights are does: the knowledge opens so many doors that may have been closed before. You now know what's needed to have a valid lien in Texas. All of the leverage is yours.

You run a successful business, and one of the key elements of a successful business is collecting the money you are owed. Contractors are fortunate that they do have ways of securing the amounts they are owed. Just imagine all of those companies out there that do not have these rights; if their customer goes out of business, they are just out of luck. But not you. As a contractor, you can secure your right to payment and collect from other parties than the one that hired you. We have gone over the rules and actions required to secure the amounts you are owed, but let's review them briefly.

CHAPTER 1: CREDIT IN THE CONSTRUCTION INDUSTRY

The entire construction industry runs on credit. Understanding liens is essential to running a profitable construction business.

CHAPTER 2: THE FIRST STEP TO HAVING A VALID LIEN

You must know your place in the construction food chain and the type of project you are working on to know when to act to have a valid lien.

CHAPTER 3: NOTICES, NOTICES, NOTICES

The most important part of having a valid lien is sending the right notice at the right time the right way to the right people and being able to prove that you did it.

CHAPTER 4: HOW TO FILE A VALID LIEN

Homestead, residential, and constitutional liens require the earliest action.

CHAPTER 5: HOW TO FILE A VALID LIEN

Just when you thought you knew something...There's so much more to consider with commercial projects.

CHAPTER 6: THE LIEN FORM

This must be done to a T, or your lien will be no good.

CHAPTER 7: HOW TO FILE A VALID BOND CLAIM

Know what to do to collect your money on government-backed projects before you begin work.

CHAPTER 8: WHAT CLAIMS DO I HAVE ON A FEDERAL PROJECT?

What a hot mess.

CHAPTER 9: I DID NOT GET PAID; CAN I TAKE MY STUFF BACK?

Yes, no, maybe. It depends.

CHAPTER 10: SPECIALLY FABRICATED MATERIALS

You can have a lien for custom-made materials even if they are not used or delivered to the project.

CHAPTER 11: HOW TO COLLECT RETAINAGE EVERY TIME

It is possible to collect retainage every time, but you will have to file a lien.

CHAPTER 12: HOW TO ENFORCE YOUR LIEN

Sometimes filing your lien is not enough to collect your money. Know what your options are if this happens to you.

CHAPTER 13: COMMON DEFENSES TO LIENS

If you know what someone will say to attempt to defect your lien, you can do a better job of preemptively documenting these things during the project.

CHAPTER 14: BONDS ON PRIVATE PROJECTS

How can a bond on a private project affect your lien rights?

CHAPTER 15: LIEN WAIVERS AND LIEN RELEASES

Never sign an unconditional lien waiver unless the money is already in the bank.

CHAPTER 16: HOW TO CREATE A CONSISTENT COLLECTION STRATEGY

Collections is not something you should think about for the first time when you are owed money.

Now you have the tools to run a profitable business by making sure what you are owed is collected. Go pull your open invoice report, and see what projects you can take action on now to protect your rights. If you would prefer for me to handle your liens and all collection issues for one flat rate, visit **subcontractorinstitute.com.**

GLOSSARY OF KEY TERMS

breach of contract claim: A claim brought in a lawsuit to collect an unsecured debt.

commercial project: All projects that are not residential, homestead, or public.

constitutional lien: A mechanic's and materialman's lien provided for by the Texas Constitution, this is only available if you have an agreement directly with the owner.

facially valid: A lien filed according to all the rules. If your lien is not facially valid, it can be removed easily.

federal project: A project that is contracted for or owned by a federal governmental entity.

homestead: A residential property that is owned by the same person that is living at the property on a full-time basis. An individual or married couple can only have one homestead at a time.

mechanic's and materialman's lien ("lien"): A piece of paper filed in the county records that secures the debt you are owed for labor and materials supplied to a project.

removable: If you have filed a statutory lien and your work can be easily removed, you can remove whatever you installed.

residential project: A single-family house, duplex, triplex, or quadruplex owned by one or more individual persons; one or more owners plan on staying there for some period of time.

retainage: 10% of the contract amount between the owner and the general contractor is required by law to be withheld by the owner for thirty days after final completion of the project. If the owner properly withholds retainage, the timeline for filing a lien is shortened to within thirty days of final completion, regardless of when you performed your work or supplied materials.

secured debt: Any type of debt whose collection is secured by an asset. If you don't pay the debt, whoever lent you the money will sell the asset to satisfy the debt.

sham contract: A mechanism that allows you to have a constitutional lien even if you don't have an agreement directly with the owner. If the general contractor and the owner are the same person, or two different companies controlled by the same person, the contract between the owner and the general contractor is considered a sham contract. In this case, it's as if you were dealing directly with the owner and you have a constitutional lien.

specially fabricated materials: Materials that are made specifically for a project and cannot really be used anywhere else.

statutory lien: A mechanic's and materialman's lien provided for by the laws of the state of Texas. A lien is available to anyone who improves private property with their labor or materials. You must comply with all the required laws to have a valid lien.

Texas public works project: A project contracted for or owned by a Texas governmental entity.

trapped funds: Funds are considered trapped when you send proper notice to the owner while they still have funds due to the general contractor. The owner is required to hold the funds until you are paid the amount you are owed, or the owner will pay you directly.

unsecured debt: Debt not secured by an asset. If you don't pay the debt, whoever lent you the money will send you to collections and have to sue you to recover the amount you owe.

ABOUT THE AUTHOR

KARALYNN CROMEENS is the founder of The Cromeens Law Firm, PLLC (TCLF). Founded in 2006, TCLF focuses on the complete representation of contractors and material suppliers. Karalynn has reviewed and negotiated thousands of subcontracts; she is on a mission to make the subcontract a fair document. The first step on this mission is to teach contractors what the terms of the subcontract mean and the risk involved with the terms so they can make informed decisions before the subcontract is signed. When Karalynn is not helping contractors and material suppliers, she enjoys spending time with her husband, Brad, and her three daughters, Lily, Holly, and Jessy.